THE CAREER MENTOR

Launch Your Career, Seize Opportunities,

Embrace Challenges And Plan For Success

JAMES TAYLOR

mindset multimedia

ISBN: 978-1-910848-57-9

Published by Mindset Multimedia Ltd

Contact:

info@mindsetmulti.media

X (formerly Twitter): @career_mindset

Facebook & LinkedIn: The Career Mentor

For

Julia and Isabella

CONTENTS

Chapter 1

Introduction

In the summer of 2018 my manager, six years my junior, swore in my face when we disagreed on the best way to prepare a demonstration that I would be presenting at a conference to over 300 people. I was due to give a walkthrough of a trading platform because the product owner's usual presenter was double-booked on the conference date and couldn't make it. Somebody else would have to do it – me. So, they trained me up on their product, and I would present it to a terrifyingly large audience despite not really knowing what the product was and with only a few weeks to familiarise myself with it. At the end of the conference, my company asked the audience to complete a feedback form about the presenters that day. I picked up a pile of forms left behind and read them. The reviews about me were absolutely damning. Some jobs can be brutal because there is nowhere to hide and no room for fear to get in your way.

There are typically two ways to learn how to swim. You either take lessons and slowly build your competence and confidence over time, or somebody throws you in the deep end, and you figure out how to keep your head above water. This job was all about going into the deep end, and I was forced to grow. In this role, you either stepped up to the big time or else you'd be shown the exit. I refused to quit.

Introductory chapters of books such as these often involve the writer attempting to assert their credibility over the book's topic. So, what is it that makes me an authority figure in the field of career navigation, and how can this book help you? I have never received any professional coaching qualification nor sat any courses on career development because I have always felt that nothing beats practical experience. I could participate in coaching programmes and then reel off lists of things I've been taught, but I'm not sure how helpful or convincing you would find that. What I do have is perhaps more important than all else: real-life, real-world experience in work across different industries, sectors and trades. I've hit brick walls, been stuck in ruts and slipped up many times. I've been rejected far more often than I care to remember and have failed in interviews, work projects and promotion opportunities multiple times. I've also had many wins, successes and accomplishments along the way.

For this book, I've taken out my magnifying glass and reviewed what worked and what did not, studying all my scars and bundling my knowledge and experience into a practical manual for your reference to help you navigate through your own journey.

So, here's a brief run-down of my journey so far. I'm someone who grew up with no clue about what to do with my life. My aspirations flicked between being a commercial airline pilot, a lawyer, a sports agent, a record label founder, a financial trader, and a screenplay writer. I felt lost a lot of the time until I finally had a breakthrough as a business leader at financial companies, from enrolling in one as an intern in my early thirties to becoming a director at another in under five years.

Before this point, I didn't have a single purpose or passion. However, I've come to learn that I have several and have found that this is, in fact, the case for most people. To those of you who've always known what you wanted from your careers, I greet you with both respect and envy.

I'm going to be authentic in what I share in this book because it will help you to believe me and place your trust in what I am writing. This way, you can learn from my experiences and transform your own fortunes. My authenticity has led to countless former colleagues asking for my advice. I get messages from folks who perceive me to be successful, confident, knowledgeable or some combination of the above. I'm not sure how true any of that is, but their reaching out for my help made me realise that if they need someone who can help them, then others probably do, too. These people ask me for advice on what to do about a certain predicament at work or about a more general conflict or challenge they are trying to overcome. I help them, and they leave with some actionable ideas on what to do about their dilemmas. They see their situation differently and feel better about it.

Career advice was offered to me at school, but it was not particularly helpful. I sat a number of tests to determine my personality type, temperament, intelligence level and so on and was presented with a bunch of careers I'd be suited to. Yet, none of them felt quite right, and the career advice I received was seldom useful. While on paper you might be able to match personality traits to certain jobs, enjoying a successful career requires a genuine interest in what you're doing every day for work. Nothing ever seemed to quite click for me.

I've read that in some countries, access to career guidance counsellors is only available through mental health clinics, which came as a bit of a shock. The kind of support that people need in relation to their careers can be very challenging to find. Therefore, this book seeks to provide some of that missing value from the career advice we receive as children and young adults because what we *really* need to understand about success in our careers is not usually shared with us at a young age. Sometimes, the advice is absent altogether. I am a descendant of two generations of doctors, so I grew up in an environment that demonstrated the importance of helping and nurturing others. Career navigation is something I can definitely help others with. At this stage of my career, I've seen and lived through enough that right now feels like the best time to pass on my knowledge to help you steer your ship, too.

An important message for you is not to stop here. This literature is not meant to be a final authority over career navigation. You should always read lots of different materials on any topic you are examining. More opinions, words of wisdom and shared lessons will help you build up an overall understanding of a topic to inform your actions. For instance, work to supplement this book with others that offer wealth-building advice and other self-help materials that align with your goals. This applies to any domain you are seeking to understand better.

Tomorrow is already here

In a world that is moving increasingly faster with the influx of technology and Artificial Intelligence (AI) exemplifying the law of accelerated returns, it has become more difficult, stressful and unsettling for people to find their place within all the ensuing chaos. Concerns have been raised over whether AI will cause unemployment across different industries and, in 2023, we are already seeing this manifesting in the form of writer's strikes in the film and television industry. An entire television series can now be created with minimal human input.

I often think back to when I was considering which subjects to study at school. Learning languages was compulsory, and I was given the option to learn a few: French, German, Spanish or Latin. For years I have joked with friends that for my child, the list of languages would look more like this: French, German, Spanish, Python, JavaScript.

I recently returned to my high school twenty years after graduating for a reunion dinner with other alumni and was fortunate enough to have been given a tour of the school by a current pupil. We were discussing the variety of subjects taught at the school today, and I discovered that not only is Python available for current pupils to learn, but it also forms a mandatory part of the curriculum up to the age of sixteen. This means the future I envisioned is already here, and sooner than I had anticipated.

Python and JavaScript are computer programming languages, and programming languages such as these underpin everything we see and use on our computers, tablets, smartphones and on the internet. They're used to 'code' (write) the software programmes we create documents on, develop mobile apps with and play video games on.

I am very envious that some children of today are being mandated to learn programming languages because it can only serve them well in our era of technology. I began learning a bit of self-taught Python a few years ago, and for those 'in the know,' I made it as far as print('Hello, world!'). If I could help my younger self, one of the things I would tell him is to learn Python or another programming language. With that, I could do all sorts of cool things like build mobile applications, trading algorithms or explore the wealth of working opportunities for people with those skills.

Maybe I'll pick up Python again one day. In the meantime, I've built a physical rather than digital application using the only language I know well – English. This physical application is of course what the old world calls a book. So, this is a book with a doff of the cap to the new digital age we have begun to evolve into.

Finally, I want to draw your attention to a tweet by someone who knows a thing or two about modern technology.

Credit: X (formerly Twitter): @elonmusk

Take a look at the middle phrase in particular. Rather than learning from my mistakes alone, I'd like to think you'll also learn from my experiences. This way, you'll be better prepared to encounter similar moments in your own life. You'll remember what is written in this book, or you can pick it up again to consult with when you're in a bit of a muddle.

This book and my experience largely stem from working at companies and building a career through experience, grit, setbacks and resilience. While the corporate world isn't for everyone, as you will see, some of the most rewarding and valuable career lessons have come from working outside of traditional companies as well. What has helped tremendously through all of these experiences is having various people I consider mentors to help guide me through them.

Finding mentors is easier said than done. I've been fortunate enough to have benefitted from the wisdom of several mentors and have consolidated what I've learnt from them here in one place. Treat this book as an opportunity to peek under the hood of the working world and what you might expect to encounter in your career. For those already making their way, you will already have experienced some ups and downs, and I hope the advice you read can help you with any further challenges that await you. The chances are that you don't have too many people with recent experience of what you're going through or knowledge of the challenges ahead to speak with. Or perhaps you do have people like mum or dad, or careers tutors at school or career advice centres who mean well but just don't seem to get you. This book will advise you without judgement or ridicule.

So, let's get to work.

Chapter 2

Getting Work Experience

Employers love hiring people with experience. It's the career equivalent to the chicken or egg dilemma – which came first? Employers want experience; employees need the employer to give it to them. This chapter looks at the types of work experience you can search for when starting out in your career or even when making a career change. We'll look into how to narrow down your career choice selection, the value of internships and work placements, and working abroad.

Earlier I mentioned my recent return to high school some twenty years after graduating. Let's go back to that time, as school is the era when most people begin considering what they want to do when they grow up. I grew up and was schooled in London, UK, with a two-year stint in Manchester during my primary (elementary) school years. I think I might be in the minority when I say this, but I look back fondly at my school years. It's not that I was keen on homework, exams or the pressure to get good grades. I didn't really enjoy that aspect. What I loved was building friendships, playing sports and dreaming about the future. And if I'm being totally frank, it was brilliant to simply enjoy life without the burden of having to pay bills and be responsible for others, something I appreciate even more now.

In the UK, most children need to consider what they will do for a career by the age of around fourteen or fifteen. This will inform which subjects they study and sit examinations for between the ages of fifteen and sixteen. Then, they would typically narrow down to three or four subjects by the age of eighteen, and those subjects will commonly relate to the subject they will read at undergraduate level at university if they opt to pursue further education at all.

I don't know what I should be doing with my life . . . HELP!

As I write this in my late thirties, the idea that children aged fifteen should know what they want to do with their lives is completely ridiculous. If you are reading this as a teenager, make sure you understand this and take some of the pressure off yourself over what you should be doing with your life. You are about to embark on an incredible quest, and this should bring excitement, not anxiety.

Most of this book is about career navigation through your twenties and thirties, but I'd be doing teenage readers a disservice to skip past their foundation-building years, so I will spend a few short pages on those first. I remember being at that age and feeling immense frustration, guilt, despair and paralysis at the fact that I didn't know what I wanted to do for a career. So, if you're reading this and are in that situation currently, the first thing I want you to know is that you absolutely do not need to worry about this. Do your best to stay calm – you are a teenager; how can you possibly know what you want to do with your life? There's no need to panic or stress over it. And by the way, there are people who still feel like this in their twenties and thirties, too!

Now, before moving on, I want to add that I went to school with several people who knew what they wanted to do for a career from when they were young, and they are doing exactly that today. However, most people I have encountered in life were not so sure. And even if you think you know what you want, you won't know if you'll actually enjoy it until you're doing it. Enjoying your work is pretty important – we'll discuss much more on that later.

If you're not sure what you want to do, you're like most people. Relax.

How do I start figuring out what I want to do for a career?

Working out what you want to do can be a messy process, especially if you need to make a decision about what to do without knowing anything about the career you're considering. The key is to understand that this is a process and that the lightbulb moment you're waiting for may take years to happen.

However, the process needs to start somewhere, so don't sit and do nothing. You need to do something to avoid getting stuck in a rut and feeling down about your situation. Keeping yourself busy will maintain your spirits and make it more likely that you'll come across something you enjoy. Many of the things we end up doing for work come as a result of trying to do something entirely different.

When pursuing an education in financial trading in my early thirties, I noticed an opening for an internship at a financial services company that I was eventually hired for. There's a connection to be drawn there in that they both fall within the remit of 'Finance,' but what began as a goal to become a self-employed trader became a career in sales, business development and commercial strategy at FinTech companies across the foreign exchange and cryptocurrency industries. I realised there would be no better way to understand how trading works than to work for the companies offering those services. Without doing something, which in this case was pursuing an education in trading, I wouldn't have discovered and been able to capitalise on the opportunity of the internship. Take some time to consider which path you want to try first and start going after it. You might find you hit a few dead ends and need to try again with something else. Finding your path can be a messy process, but you need to start somewhere.

How do I narrow my path down to a few subjects or categories?

If you want to pursue something academic after school, then you're probably looking at going to university or another institution for further studies. If you're still not 100 percent sure about what to study during further education but need to make a decision because application deadlines are looming, you should either take a gap year or look for subjects that have a broad scope of application and are future-proofed against technological advancements. These will typically include subjects such as law, communications, construction, languages (spoken and coded!), business studies and computer science to name a few.

Do I need work experience to kick-start my career?

If you're lucky, your school or college will have some career guidance available to you. They may even take you to career fairs or help you gain work placements or summer internships. If you are no longer at school or don't have those opportunities readily available, then don't worry too much about it. These things seem like a good idea but will seldom help you figure out what you *really* want from your career. While schools and colleges will try to help their students figure out what to do for a career, they can only get students so far because this is such a personal journey and one that only you can take.

When I was a student, I did a couple of weeks' worth of work experience at different companies, photocopying documents and making teas for people. At the time I was under the impression that having these experiences would look good on my limited CV. But really it was just an opportunity to look behind the curtain in a working office environment more so than getting an understanding of whether a particular company or job would be a good fit for my future. The number of jobs I was offered because of this experience? *Zero.*

That being said, there's absolutely no harm in work experience schemes. If you *know* you want to work at these companies, work experience can be a meaningful way to forge relationships with key stakeholders at an early stage. However, my experiences didn't propel me into a dream job or help me figure out what I wanted to do for my career.

How important are summer internships?

The University of Maryland describes an internship as 'a professional learning experience that offers meaningful, practical work related to a student's field of study or career interest.'* Formal summer internships have highly competitive enrolment

* https://careers.umbc.edu/employers/internships/what-is-an-internship/

processes and are few and far between. Being accepted into one is no mean feat, and although the value one can ascribe to a summer internship probably ranges wildly, they are a significant opportunity to establish and build relationships for future opportunities, as described above. It's important to note that while I'm not shooting summer internships down, *most of us will not be able to get work placements like these.* So again, don't worry if you're not able to secure one. Instead, look for other ways to develop yourself.

<u>What else can I do other than work experience schemes?</u>

'The world is a book, and those who do not travel read only one page.'

Saint Augustine

I've always been a keen traveller, and although I read this quote only recently, it resonated strongly with me. Of course, not everyone can afford travel, but I know plenty of people who would prefer a shiny new car or money spent on expensive hobbies rather than on exploring the world.

Career growth is as much about personal development as it is about notching up the years you work in a job and becoming a master of your trade. Extended periods of travel force you to discover the world and grow as a person. This is even more important today when internationalisation and globalisation permeate many, if not most, industries. There are lots of people who spend years and years in a job but never seem to go anywhere with their careers. Then there are others who seem to fly and perform well wherever they go. The key distinction between those examples is character and tenacity, both of which are enhanced by travelling to new places. It is also very helpful to forge new connections with people in your career network when you can use places you have travelled to as an area of mutual interest.

Thinking back to the short-term jobs I've worked, some of those that developed me as a person the most were the ones I worked abroad. The beauty of working abroad is that you can explore the world and gain valuable character-building experience at the same time. Having a strong and likeable character will help you attract career opportunities.

What kind of work should I look for?

Aside from the possibility of connecting with hiring managers during a summer placement in an office, how does a placement build your character? I'm not convinced that it does to any great degree. And in any case, most people won't have access to opportunities like these. So, when I've been asked about work experience by young aspiring professionals, the focus is on personal growth more than anything, and they're probably disappointed when I advise them to find work in a kitchen. Yes, you read that correctly.

How will kitchen work help me in a career outside of catering?

First, a basic job cleaning dishes and surfaces in a kitchen and completing simple tasks like food prep for the chefs is open to more or less anybody. These jobs require no prior experience. Summer placements and internships are usually reserved for people from certain schools or universities, perhaps with certain grades, and for every position going there are hundreds of applicants. What can the 99 per cent of people who won't be afforded such opportunities do productively with their time? The entry requirements for a 'dish pig' – the jargon used for this job in Australia – are as low as they come. Anybody capable of actively moving around a kitchen can clean dishes and carry out simple food prep.

You will additionally experience so much while working in a kitchen. It can be a busy, stressful working environment. There is usually a demanding head chef who exemplifies a desire for perfectionism in their work. Time sensitivity is appreciated as food cannot be served cold. Learning to work as a team is necessary, as everyone in the kitchen has a role that interacts in some way with other staff during a dining session. Customers are hungry, and there is pressure to deliver food that tastes good. Fast.

The bonds I formed in kitchens were among the best I've ever forged. Working in a kitchen teaches you incredible life lessons, and I'd recommend it to anybody. I worked in kitchens in Australia, as above, and also at a kids' summer camp in the USA with a bunch of other people from different backgrounds and nationalities. Both jobs were, hands down, some of the best experiences of my life.

We see the dining area of a restaurant when eating out, but rarely behind the door to the kitchen. Behind that door is a world of conflict and varying degrees of chaos, tension, pressure, perfectionism, camaraderie and teamwork, spearheaded by a manager (the head chef) and a team of people pulling together to drive results. These are all ingredients for personal growth and strong character. Whichever path you decide to take moving forward, you will have been exposed to a working environment you will most likely encounter many times in your life.
When interviewing for a job, you're often asked to give examples of a time when you worked under pressure or as a team. If you've worked in a kitchen, you will be able to provide an example of a

time when you worked under pressure, to tight deadlines, as a team and with pressure to perform.

Similar rules apply to working in catering and hospitality in general. I spent seven priceless months in Australia juggling three jobs over a six-day working week (Thursday was my weekend), which included waiting tables, serving celebrities in corporate suites at a sports stadium and being a "dish pig" in a pub. Hollywood actors often famously start out by waiting tables before making their audition breakthroughs, and even many successful CEOs began their careers in catering.

Tej Lalvani · 3rd+ + Follow ···
CEO of Vitabiotics & Dragon on BBC's Dragons' Den (2...
6mo ·

People often ask me what it takes to become a CEO, and my answer is always the same - it's the journey, not just the destination.

It's a well-known fact that I started my career at McDonald's and am proud of it. Unfortunately, it seems that these days, many people are ashamed of their humble beginnings, particularly if it involves working in the service industry. I'm here to tell you there is no shame in working hard and starting from the bottom.

My time at McDonald's taught me the value of hard work, teamwork, and customer service. I learned to handle difficult situations, stay calm under pressure, and always keep a positive attitude.

These are all qualities that have contributed immensely to who I am today and have helped me to succeed in my career.

So, if you're at the start of your career or find yourself in a job that you're not entirely happy with, remember that every stop along the way is an opportunity to learn and grow.

Every experience, no matter how big or small, plays a role in shaping who you are and what you can achieve.

Credit: LinkedIn: Tej Lalvani

Never be ashamed to tell anyone about your job, no matter how small you perceive it to be. You are on your journey, making your way and shaping your future self. There is no shame in that.

There will be kitchens and hospitality opportunities in your home country, and those character-building moments will be found there too. However, I found it particularly helpful to undergo this work abroad in Australia and the USA. This is where I got to explore the world while working and take myself away from the comfort zone of home, leading to the personal growth and character-building experiences that made me who I am today. I have friends who found it useful to do the same but in countries where the native language was different to their own, in order to pursue their ambition of becoming bi-lingual.

Yes, Chef. How do I find out more about working abroad?

If you're taking a gap year after school, then you have ample opportunity to find work abroad. If you're a student, especially in the UK and Europe, the Camp-America-type programmes are a great way to find summer work abroad in an English-speaking country.* It's also relatively easy to obtain a work visa from the American embassy because they know you're returning to a full-time programme of study at home. At the time of writing,

* https://www.campamerica.com/

Australia has a working holiday visa for eighteen to thirty-five year-olds from many countries around the world.[*] For my Australian and New Zealand readers down under, the UK offers a reciprocal scheme for you.[□]

[*] https://immi.homeaffairs.gov.au/what-we-do/whm-program/overview
[□] https://www.gov.uk/youth-mobility

KEY TAKEAWAYS:

OK, so we've discussed a few things in this chapter, from figuring out what to do for your career to gaining the work experience that employers so often seek from candidates. Here's a summary of what we've covered so far:

- Most people don't know what they want to do with their lives, especially early on in their careers. If this is you, what you're experiencing is normal and not cause for alarm
- Start pursuing something you find interesting. You'll be amazed by how things fall into place once you begin to apply yourself to something new
- Work experience relating to professions is difficult to come by and highly competitive. Seek out other opportunities with low barriers of entry to grow your skill set
- Working abroad takes you out of your comfort zone and can help to fast-track your growth and personal development

Chapter 3

Excelling at Interviews

Before receiving a job offer, you are almost certainly going to be assessed. This assessment will come in the form of one or more interviews but may also include additional assessments or tests. Understanding interviews and being able to excel at them is critical to career success. Therefore, this chapter will explore some of the key aspects surrounding interviews, such as how to get them, prepare for them, perform in them and receive a job offer.

What are some of the ways to secure an interview?

Before we discuss interviews themselves, let's first spend some time exploring how to get them. I'm generalising a little here, but interviews most often come about as a result of one of the following four ways:

1) A company posts a job vacancy on a job or careers portal (this could be their own portal or a public one) that lists the specifications of the job itself and the skills, qualifications and experience they are looking for in candidates.

2) The candidate does not know if companies are hiring, so they send their CV and cover letter to as many as possible in their field in the hope that someone reads them.

3) A head-hunter or recruiter assesses your profile and deems you to be a good fit for a vacancy they are being paid to fill.

4) A person has developed a network, and contact is made through an acquaintance or connection about a position.

I have found work through all four of these examples, so I can confidently say that all options are viable. Now let's examine them in more detail:

1) Job or careers portals

Although I have found this to be a painful way of finding a job, I got one of the most rewarding job opportunities of my life through this process. The reason it is painful is because it is extremely time-consuming and usually bears no fruit. You can spend hours applying for job after job, trying to make your application paint you in the best light possible, only to not hear anything back. It very quickly feels like the juice isn't worth the squeeze.

Another thing to add is that job hunting is extremely competitive, so human resources and hiring managers are extremely fickle with the applications received. If something on your CV doesn't meet the standards in the job advertisement, it's likely your application goes in the bin along with your CV and cover letter. If one hundred people are applying for one job, and fifty of them do not have the grades required or minimum degree score specified, then the recruiter can shred your application safe in the knowledge there's probably a good fit among the remaining fifty candidates. Additionally consider that the people reviewing the CVs and applications have other duties at work and simply cannot afford the time to go through every application with a fine-toothed comb. They will sift through inbound applications ruthlessly.

Another common issue is that many jobs are posted online because it's HR policy to do so, but the company's intention is to hire or promote internally. When this is the case, it means that one hundred out of one hundred applications go straight into the bin. If each applicant spends three hours crafting their perfect application, that means three hundred hours were collectively wasted by all applicants. Pretty harsh, right?

It's a tedious and disheartening process, and you have my sympathies if you can relate to it. We've all been there. However, as I mentioned, I did find an amazing career opportunity by applying this way, which goes to show that if you can persevere and commit to the time needed to grind through applications, the likelihood of something going your way increases. Don't forget that by sharing your CV with an employer, you will be retained on their database for future opportunities, too.

2) Cold-selling your cover letter and CV

This is another gruelling process. After graduating from university, I was looking for work in sports management. I went on to Google and searched for sports management agencies that were commutable from where I lived. From the resulting shortlist, I browsed their websites and then adapted my CV and cover letter to appear suited to roles at each one. I posted by mail (those were the days) both documents blindly and addressed them as 'Dear Sir or Madam,' not knowing who worked there or whether my documents would even be read.

For a while, I didn't hear back from anybody. Then, one day, I received a call from the CEO of one of the agencies. He was considering hiring someone to help out in future and just wanted to establish initial contact with no promises made. This was a huge breakthrough for me, as someone had picked up my letter and responded. I happened to really like this company, and although I didn't hear from them again for several months, I emailed the CEO periodically to let him know what I was up to. I was studying for a postgraduate qualification in sports law at the time and told him what I was learning and how I envisaged that knowledge becoming beneficial to his business. I retained a keen interest to one day work with him. He never replied to me, but I kept emailing him every few months regardless in the hope that something might open up for me. And it did. He eventually called me in for an interview, and I worked there for two years. The moral of the story is to cast a wide net and keep persisting with those who make contact. The more people you reach out to, the more likely it is someone will bite.

3) Head-hunters and recruiters

I have met both excellent recruiters and extremely disappointing ones. The latter I find to be self-serving and more like typical, sleazy salespeople. They fail to take a real interest in the candidates. Although their pay is heavily commission-based, and they do need to be ruthless to an extent, I believe it is possible to find a balance between looking out for oneself and striking a good relationship and rapport with candidates. The good recruiters I've worked with are truly exceptional people. The bad ones, not so much. The recruitment industry is quite polarised in this regard. Recruiters are paid when their candidate is employed by their employing client, so they need to screen candidates efficiently when attempting to fit well-suited people to the jobs they are tasked with hiring for. As with above, don't forget that your CV will be retained on file for future opportunities if nothing comes from the most recent contact.

Another thing to consider is that *your* pay can be affected if you gain work through a recruiter. Head-hunter costs are high, so the budget for your role will be split between you and the recruiter who gains a commission for hiring you. For this reason, you can receive better pay through having direct communication with the employer rather than going through a middleman.

Additionally, this is something to consider when negotiating pay, as you can ask for more when a recruiter is not involved because the employer doesn't have to apportion their budget for the role to more than one person.

One caveat to this is where an employer has an in-house recruitment team. In this situation, the monetary conflict of interest described above is absent because the recruiter is already being compensated as an employee. In-house recruiters are paid to hunt for hiring candidates, so keep your LinkedIn profile up-to-date, along with any other job portals you use. You never know who is looking at your profile and your next big opportunity might be just around the corner.

4) Network

Your network is an interconnected group of people in which you are the common denominator. This network will include friends, family, people you associate with professionally and other acquaintances. Your network will grow organically as your career advances, but you can enhance this growth by attending social and networking events. Very often, these events will be industry-specific, meaning that there will be a higher concentration of people who might be able to help you further down the road.

By gradually building a network, you will find that opportunities become more readily available to you. Perhaps you worked with someone in a job who later hires for something you'd be well-suited for. They have already worked with you, so they know your skillset and temperament and deem you a good fit. Or perhaps they themselves are not the person hiring, but their friend or acquaintance is, and so they connect you to them. This is a luxury you can enjoy when you have established yourself and your reputation.

Can you give me some tips on how to produce a good CV?

Your CV should be a one- or two-page summary of your work experience and qualifications. There are plenty of resources on the internet about how to produce a good CV, and you can also consult professional CV-enhancing services. Having been a hiring manager and reviewed hundreds of CVs, below are some key aspects to consider:

- Short, concise summaries are helpful as a busy hiring manager has other duties
- Good flow and easy-to-read formats are much appreciated. Instead of using small fonts to cram more in, try to deliver the same content in fewer words
- Highlight your skills but remember it can be obvious and therefore disadvantageous if you've over-tweaked your CV to suit the role better
- Anything over two pages gets you off to a bad start
- If your CV and experience aren't suited to the role, don't apply

What can I expect from my first few interviews?

You're likely to begin your career in what the working world calls an 'entry-level' position. In an entry-level position, you have little to nothing to offer experience-wise, and with that comes a relatively weak bargaining position. Therefore, employers must assess you on other factors to decide whether you're worth investing in. And make no mistake, it's important to understand that you're an investment for them. Your hands-on skill is likely limited if not completely lacking, so educating and training you will cost your employer both time and valuable company resources before you begin providing a return on their investment through your performance. At this point, you want to gain interview experience to understand how they flow and what it feels like to be in the spotlight. As you complete more interviews, your performance in them will improve, and you'll begin to convince employers you are worth investing in.

What makes for a good performance at interview?

You will need to interview for most of the jobs you apply for. This is how an employer gets to know you. It's an assessment of your competency, knowledge and skills, as well as their way of judging whether you're a good cultural fit for them. No two interviews are ever the same, but they do tend to follow the same core aspects.

Do your research

You must research the company you're interviewing for. This is non-negotiable. I have interviewed many candidates, and one of the most annoying traits is a lack of basic research into the company they're seeking employment from. I shouldn't even need to write this, but because of the sheer number of people I've interviewed who clearly didn't do their homework, I need to lay it out clearly. Go to the employer's website and find out about their products and services. Check their recent press releases and understand the history of the company and its evolution. Discover who the founders are, what the company's vision is and what the competitive landscape looks like. So few people complete this preparation that by doing it, you're already putting yourself at an advantage over other candidates. And it's a really simple, basic and obvious thing to do.

Be Authentic

Authenticity is the quality of being genuine. Be yourself! Show your interviewer who you really are, that you have a likeable personality, how your mind works and what makes you tick. They will appreciate it, and it will help distinguish you from other people who are trying to say what they think the interviewer wants to hear. If you can be yourself, it will project that you have confidence and belief in yourself.

Being an authentic person makes the other person think you're believable and honest, as it's difficult to fake authenticity and easy to spot or feel when someone is being disingenuous, making them more difficult to trust.

Demonstrate that you can get along with others

You are likely to spend thirty-five to forty hours per week, if not more, with your colleagues. A grossly underestimated part of the interview process is the fact that you could be working with these people, and they with you, for most of your waking hours during the week. It's a lot of time to spend together! So it's vital that you get along with each other.

It's important not to force a connection, so do make sure you read the room, but attempt to find a way of getting along with the people you're going to be working with.* Find a mutual interest or common ground during interview small talk. Where are they from? Where have they travelled to? Did they work somewhere previously that you know something about? Perhaps you know one of their colleagues. Keep politics, religious beliefs and anything divisive out of the conversation and find a way to connect and build rapport with them. Remember, you are inviting yourself into their family, and being likeable and getting along with others demonstrates you can be a good cultural fit.

---

* When interning at one job, my manager at the time personally purchased the book "How to Win Friends and Influence People" by Dale Carnegie for me. I recommend reading it for more on getting along with others.

Smile!

It naturally follows that you should smile when seeking to get along with the interviewers. Your facial expressions and mannerisms should transmit a happy, positive energy. Be a fun, friendly, happy and motivating influence on the room and your future colleagues, even if those things are not being reciprocated back to you. If you are interviewing by telephone, smile then, too. Smiling has been scientifically proven[1] to produce endorphins in the brain (the 'feel-good' hormones), and this will reflect in your tone of voice and help transmit positive energy through the phone line.

Train yourself to be comfortable with silent pauses

Sometimes you will be asked difficult questions. I find some of the most difficult ones to be the behavioural or situational-type questions. *Tell me about a time when you dealt with pressure. Tell me about a time when you had to work as a team. Tell me about a time when you had to work with a deadline.* You might be thinking, 'If only I'd worked in a kitchen!'

---

[1] https://www.ted.com/talks/ron_gutman_the_hidden_power_of_smiling/transcript?language=en

The purpose of situational questions is to gain insight into how a candidate handles challenging situations. You will find many articles online that provide great examples of situational questions and answers. You can prepare some of these and learn them as a script beforehand

However, the best way to answer these questions lies not in the answers themselves but in your calmness and composure. You've been put on the spot, the silence in the room is deafening, and you can feel the pressure to find an answer. This is the moment you can demonstrate how well you really do handle pressure.

Your reflex might be to quickly blurt something out to fill the silence and answer the question. But would it not be more impressive if you were to sit back, take a deep breath and scour your mind at your own pace for a good answer? Try to envisage what that silence looks and feels like beforehand. Ten seconds of silence feels like a lifetime in an interview room. But if you can demonstrate you are OK with it and remain composed and comfortable in the silence, you portray yourself as a person who is measured and in control. This will probably carry you further than any answer you give. Take a moment now to count to ten and imagine how long that would feel in an interview after having been asked a difficult question.

Take your time answering questions. Composure is key, and indeed some of the best interviews I had in terms of my performance were for jobs I didn't really want. Why? Because I was calm and in control – not being worried too much about the outcome meant there was a lack of pressure, enabling me to maintain my composure.

Answer the question you've been asked

I spoke to a student recently who interviewed and was rejected for a place at Oxford University because they incensed the interviewer by providing an answer to a question that wasn't posed.

Answer the interviewer's questions directly. If you don't know something, own up. Do not try to deceive the interviewer with a made-up answer or give an answer to another question that they haven't asked. They will know what you are doing and might feel offended or betrayed because you're trying to pull the wool over their eyes. They will see through it and judge you accordingly. Better to say you don't know and move on, or admit you are not sure and ask if they would like you to discuss another matter that you do know about.

Interviews are bilateral

During interviews in your early years, you are most likely going to try to impress the employer enough just to give you a job offer. Later on in your career, once you have built up some experience and reputation and know what you want from a job, you may experience a perception shift about interviews. Once you are experienced and sought after, you should consider that the interview is bilateral. That means it's a two-way conversation. They are seeking an ideal candidate, and you are seeking the right kind of job for *you*. The result is that you are interviewing them as much as they are you. This is where you come prepared with questions about the employer.

Prepare some questions for the end of the interview

The questions you will ask will depend on the job, industry and place of work you are interviewing for. Some of the things I typically ask include:

- What is a typical day in the role like?
- Who will I be working with? What is the team or department like?
- Are you experiencing any obstacles or challenges at the moment?

- What is the company's high-level vision and plan for the next one to five years?
- What will the expectations be of me during the first three months, six months and one year?
- Is the work remote, in-person or a hybrid of the two?
- What are some of the benefits offered to employees, like holidays, social events, health insurance, pension schemes, etc? (Only ask these in interviews with HR)
- What is the path for progress, promotion and increased responsibility for someone who takes a job like the one I'm interviewing for?

Ask the last question at the end of the interview to leave a positive impression of yourself, and don't forget to thank them for their time and wish them well for the remainder of their interview process. It is common courtesy to follow up with the interviewer by email in the following day or two to thank them for their time.

How long does the interview process take?

The entire interview process can take days to several months, depending on the size of the employer. Hiring new employees often involves a team of hiring managers, HR managers and other team leaders who can all be involved in the interview process. If a recruiter is involved, this would add an additional layer to the conversation sequence. My personal record is eight rounds of interviews over three or four months with an outcome of no job offer. I've also been offered a job after seven rounds of interviews spanning a period of five months. I've heard of six or even twelve-month hiring cycles. It's important to understand that these things take time, and it doesn't serve you in any way to fret about it. You shouldn't chase people excessively or harass them because you'll come across as desperate, which is off-putting. The process needs to run its course, and there's little you can do to expedite it. If you try to force it, you risk harming your chances.

Finally, many companies use consensus-based hiring, which is a process whereby different team members, managers and stakeholders at the company interview the candidates. Making a bad hire is costly for the company, so casting a large web of interviewers reduces this risk. Individually, each interviewer provides their own feedback, and collectively, they hire a candidate through mutual consensus. This can also lengthen the hiring process. It's important to remain calm, and you can do so by being in a job already or by also pursuing other work opportunities so your eggs are not all in one basket.

KEY TAKEAWAYS:

In this chapter we looked at the different ways you can seek out job opportunities. Your entry into a new job will most likely depend on passing an interview process, and the likelihood of that will be determined by a number of factors. Furthermore, we have discussed the following points:

- You can find job opportunities using career portals, by cold-sending your CV and cover letter to employers, by using recruiters or through your network
- The reviewing of candidates is a ruthless process, and your CV (and cover letter) will create a first impression
- In the interview, ensure you have researched the employer. Smile, be authentic, build rapport and remember that composure and body language go a long way
- Eventually, you will notice that your interviews become bilateral – you are interviewing them as much as they are interviewing you
- Manage your expectations regarding the hiring timeline – the interview process carries a lot of uncertainty and can take a long time

Chapter 4

Climbing the Career Ladder

Congratulations! You have successfully navigated your way through the interview process, the first hurdle facing most people at the start of a new job or career. Most people envisage a career that progresses over time. An ascension from junior roles to senior ones, and with that, promotions, pay rises and a respected reputation.

Now that you've got a foot in the door let's look at what career progression means and what's required to start making it happen. This chapter will look at some behavioural qualities you'll need to display, how to apply yourself when faced with some of the hurdles you're likely to face, how to develop your skills and some of the inner mindset challenges you'll need to conquer.

What attitude should I have when starting a new job or career?

Your attitude when starting a new job or career is crucial. I don't mean that you need to be a positive bundle of joy every day (although that helps!), but rather, your attitude is how you manage your own expectations and apply yourself. Focus your attitude on your work rather than making money, especially from the outset. Focusing on money too early in your career will make you impatient, skew your expectations, and ultimately slow your progression because your energy is in the wrong place – you are looking to cut corners and won't be able to.

If you've started a job at entry level and are only focused on being one of the best-paid employees at the company straight away, you're in for disappointment. You're going to have to earn those stripes, and even then, things like nepotism, career politics, changing industry climates and other unforeseeable events could prevent you from getting there. Instead of fixating on money, focus on having the right mindset, getting better at what you do and building knowledge. This will get you noticed and indirectly open the doors to better money-making opportunities at work further down the line. Remember: people won't pay you well unless you demonstrate you have the qualities and skills worth paying good compensation for, so focus on becoming that version of yourself first.

Working on or in something you find fun will really help you have the right attitude. Ideally, you want to see work as play. Something that you are excited to get out of bed for and have a curiosity about. Learning more about something is way more fun and easier when you *want* to rather than because you *need* to.

Your idea of fun work will likely differ from mine and be unique to you. However, to find a job interesting, you must have a fascination with the underlying product, service, business, skills or subject. This will help you harness the enthusiasm and motivation to grow, learn and excel in your role. Then, the money will flow naturally as you progress throughout your career.

This book is not a wealth management guidance tool, so I'll keep the money-making talk brief, but it is absolutely a topic worth studying further. While attitude is key, you can optimise money-making opportunities by staying loyal to those who treat you well and by aligning closely with the most valuable and highest revenue generating divisions at your employer. This is because salary and/or bonuses are likely to be better when working within the teams that generate the most revenue. Alternatively, if big salaries are important to you, research professions that are notorious for paying well.

How do I make myself popular at work?

'It's nice to be important, but it's more important to be nice. Being nice and kind to people is literally the easiest thing to do.'

Dwayne Johnson

By being nice, you make it much easier for people to like you. Your popularity will depend on how you are with other people and how dependable, flexible and versatile you can be for your superiors and colleagues. And, of course, at the very least, you will need to be competent in your work.

Although building relationships with people at work is very important, one valuable lesson I've learnt is that *a job is not a popularity contest.* One of the challenges of getting things done and displaying competence in your work is encountering different people and teams whose interests, goals and objectives conflict with your own. There are times when you will need to make difficult decisions and let people down. I've been guilty of trying to please everybody I work with. The issue is that you're shooting yourself in the foot if pleasing someone else is to your own detriment. However, do note that this is not a licence to be rude. It's perfectly possible to emit kindness, class and dignity while simultaneously making difficult decisions to fulfil the duties set by your superiors.

What is required to be considered 'experienced'?

Here's the bad news: experience pays, and there are no shortcuts to being 'experienced.' How can there be? To be experienced, you need to first encounter those experiences and come out the other side of them. You can then demonstrate your solutions to problems and make yourself more valuable to the higher-ups. Experiences mould you as a person and help you learn from your mistakes and accomplishments. You can analyse what you did right and what you did wrong. Then, when you encounter similar situations in future, you know how to handle them.

Have you ever been in the frustrating position where you want to apply for a job but it asks for two to five years' experience from candidates, and you don't have that experience? *If only someone would just take a chance on you and give you the experience you need to get some leverage.* If you apply for those jobs without the requisite experience, your application is more than likely going in the bin. This is what I meant when saying there are no shortcuts to experience. If you constantly find yourself looking at career opportunities that require more experience than you can offer, then you are looking at the wrong opportunities. Reassess your searches and investigate what roles would help you establish the experience you are looking for.

How do I start to accumulate experience?

When you are just starting out and have no experience in a field, the only option is to start with the first rung on the ladder. This means looking for internships, traineeships and junior or entry-level jobs. These are the positions that feed into the career hierarchy. We already discussed the risk an employer takes on you as a new employee. The formative period of your career is about being trained in the field in which you want to work. It's the time when you learn to ply your trade. This happens either through internal training sessions or hands-on work, and you will begin to understand how your employer functions, what their objectives are and how you fit into achieving them. This is how you begin to rack up your experience. You will be naïve and make mistakes. That's OK. This is the best time to make those mistakes and gain experience. The advantage of making mistakes during this period is that you are forgiven for doing so. This is less so the case when you're in a more senior role. Don't be too hard on yourself when making mistakes early on in your career – it is a valuable way to learn.

A lot of jobs start with a probation period – what is that?

Probation usually refers to the early stage of a new job, where you have a final practical interview before you are considered a permanent and fully onboarded member of the team. Consider it a trial process. During your probation, you will undergo training, and managers will be on the lookout to confirm their hopes that you are both competent and a good cultural fit. In employment contracts, probation is usually covered in its own clause, and your rights under the contract are somewhat limited while you earn your place as a permanent employee. Limitations in your employment contract might materialise in the form of your pay – which may be lower during probation – your ability to take holidays, and also the notice period in which either party can give to terminate the employment arrangement – this might be one week as opposed to one month during normal employment, for example.

How can I survive probation?

Whether or not you are subject to a probationary period, the first few months of a new job should be enacted in a certain way. This is a time to keep your head down, lay low and get to work. That's not to say you should hide from everyone, but you should definitely keep a low profile and avoid rustling feathers or stepping on people's toes. You are new, so you need to feel the place out, figure out who everyone is, earn their respect and discover what your colleagues do and how that interacts with your own responsibilities. Who are the bosses or other key figures in management? This period is about survival. You do not necessarily need to make a flying impact. You can survive your probation with the right attitude and by proving your competence and desire to learn.

It goes without saying, but you want to show everyone the best version of yourself. Don't show up at work hungover. Get sleep, rest well, be clean and smell good (but don't overdo the parfum). Learn as much as you can about your job, the company and its people.

Successful navigation through probation will largely depend on the role in which you are working. In some instances, it is merely a box-checking exercise for HR at the firm; in others, it is a crucial part of what will be a high-pressure job. I have experienced both. For the former, you will obviously want to make a good impression and do the simple things correctly – show up to work on time, respect your new colleagues, and show enthusiasm and attention to detail. For the latter, you will need to work 'as if your life depends on it,' as one manager once told me.

This will lead to a shift in attitude and will push you to get up to speed fast, as well as demonstrate to management your eagerness and seriousness about wanting the job. Make notes about your company and its products or services. Treat it as though you are studying for an exam. Your colleagues will be impressed if you can demonstrate you have learnt from the education they are providing you because you are treating it like a critical learning exercise. If you need to, spend time during evenings and weekends getting up to scratch. This most likely won't be necessary once you have established yourself, but if you have a very clear target to reach within a specified time, then you will need to maximise the time available to ensure you reach or exceed the standards required.

Will targets or goals be set for me during my probation?

Probation periods in which you must prove something beyond basic competency and cultural compatibility before you are awarded a permanent contract are what I call 'make or break' probations. For example, a salesperson will have to onboard a certain number of new clients by the end of their probation or generate a certain amount of revenue through sales at the same time. If the targets are met, the reward is a contract of permanent employment. If not, the employer can terminate the employment arrangement.

How can I further develop my skills during employment?

There are many companies that offer further training beyond the basics you need to learn for your day-to-day role. This is a great way to supplement the experience you are accumulating and to experience new things concurrently. I've heard a lot of people who complain about the fact their companies don't offer further training, so if this is important to you, ensure you find out about additional training programmes that might be open to you as an employee when researching the company and during your interview, when you can ask what some of the company benefits for employees are. Some companies I've worked for have offered brilliant training programmes for employees. Learning new languages, project management, managing other people and advanced training for specific roles such as computing skills. Very often, these are performed by external providers and can be an excellent way for you to become more rounded in your work and put yourself in a better position for future promotion opportunities or other job offers.

There's so much new information when starting a new job!

There will be times when you feel overwhelmed at work. Being new to something is hard when you have a heap of tasks to complete and don't know how to do them. Everyone else around you seems slick and well-versed in the job. It can feel like you have a mountain to climb, and it's quite unnerving. Any qualifications you required to get the job mean nothing now. They may have helped you to get the job itself, but because you have no practical implementation skills, it can feel like you know nothing.

This is normal! It's perfectly fine to feel a little spooked by it all. Stick at it. Get to work. As time passes, you'll feel like you're understanding things a little better and will soon feel like you're getting the hang of it. It might not feel like you're progressing much on a day-to-day basis. But at every three-month interval, look at the prior three months, and you'll realise how much things are coming together. And by that point, you'll be confident in continuing to make progress in the next three months. Using this self-imposed three-month reflection process really helps to ease the pressure of starting a new job. Also, when you start a new job in future, you know this cycle of learning will repeat itself, and it won't feel so daunting the next time; early jitters are all part of being new, and everyone goes through it. No big deal.

It's also possible to be overwhelmed by having too many tasks, too much work on your plate and too many people contacting you. Your days might be packed with back-to-back meetings, meaning you have even less time to get on top of your work. One manager once advised me to prioritise my task list and then complete them one by one. If you try to do everything all at once, you risk spreading yourself too thin and not doing anything to a good enough standard.

Where can I discover my motivating drivers?

To push through barriers in your career, you will need to find something that drives you so that you're never satisfied with what you have.

I had one job where my probation included the requirement to give a demonstration of the company's technology to the whole office, with every department in attendance. It was daunting, to say the least. I remember feeling sick on the commute to work in the mornings leading up to that day. My stomach was churning. I wanted the job badly, and I simply had to succeed in my probation. My manager at the time told me he could see the same need to succeed in me as he had when he was interning. If you really want to pass probation and succeed in the job – if you *need* it - failure simply won't be an option for you. It wasn't for me, and I hit my probation targets with a few weeks to run on my probation period and was made a full-time permanent employee shortly after.

Different people have different drives. But it's uncanny the number of successful people I've met with a chip on their shoulder. Maybe you have something to prove to yourself or someone else. Perhaps somebody said something to you that stuck with you forever, or you have a parent who you can never seem to satisfy. French football legend Thierry Henry once said, 'The greatest pressure I had in my career was putting a smile on my father's face.' Whatever it is, your drive means you become engrossed in the desire to succeed at whatever it is you are doing and to prove your worth.

I went to law school because law can open doors to many different career options. Another contributory factor towards my decision to study law was a line in one of my schoolteacher's reports to my parents in which he wrote I would 'never achieve the grades needed to get into law school.' I was enraged and couldn't believe he wrote that. It put a chip on *my* shoulder and gave me all the motivation I needed to prove myself. Another example of where I channelled anger into motivation was when I was annoyed at myself for not scoring high enough grades in certain legal exams and decided I needed to set the record straight in a later legal qualification I obtained. I ranked top of the class and was awarded a prize by the university.

Find that chip on your shoulder and use it to your advantage. But use it well. Don't turn into a jerk - that's easy to do, especially if you work in the rat race of a big city where everyone seems rude and selfish. You will stand out more if you have the chip on your shoulder that drives you but are also able to stay classy and respectful.

We will get into ego in more depth later, but I'd like to add that while it's important to keep your ego on a leash, a little bit of anger or pride can sometimes be harnessed to your advantage. Anger can drive you to push yourself harder to accomplish your goals. I'd like to talk later about tracking inspirational people, but now is a good time to share a message from someone who still uses rejection to motivate him today:

Dwayne The Rock Johnson
27 June 2022

Why I wear #54.

There are 53 men on an @NFL roster who ball out on Sundays and live their dreams.

I was #54.

I was that player who was told, "you're good, but you're not good enough...
.. thank you for all your hard work and this is where it all ends."

When you worked, lived and breathed a lifetime for something you were so passionate about, only to be told you're not good enough and there's nothing you can do it about.

Hurts.

It became one of the biggest kicks in the gut I ever got and one of the biggest mental health challenges of my life.

But as painful as it was to accept the dream is over — it also created a hunger, intensity and it gave me the biggest fucking chip on my shoulder to attack life with a relentless ferocity.

This is why #54 on my back is so deeply personal to me.

Grit, resolve, ferocity, passion, relentlessness.

Life is much different for me these days and I'm forever grateful, but that chip never goes away.

Ever.

dj
#54
#fiftyfuckingfour

Credit: Instagram: therock

Why does my motivation wax and wane?

Motivation is fleeting. I can recall several instances where I felt highly motivated towards a specific goal. However, that motivation only ever carried me so far. I have a list of almost-accomplishments. Things I started but never finished. I used the motivation to get started, but eventually, the motivation waned. And so did my commitment to see things through. It took many almost-accomplishments to realise that motivation is, more often than not, temporary.

The crucial lesson to learn here is that you must respect the fact that motivation is temporary, and that the qualities that will carry you to the finish line are dedication, commitment and consistency. If you rely solely on motivation, you'll often find you fail to meet the achievements you set out for. I wish I had learnt this lesson sooner, as when I now feel motivated about something, I appreciate in advance that my motivation is unlikely to last. With this in mind, I can manage my commitment towards a project, safe in the knowledge that I will need to persist long after the motivation dies.

How can I find a mentor beyond this book?

Find a mentor, they say. But who is this mystical person who is supposed to appear out of the mist, take us under their wing and hold our hand as we navigate through life? There are a few people who are fortunate enough to find that inspiring person: a retiree who wants to give something back to a young buck or the Godfather of a business empire who wants to hand over the keys to a prodigal son. The concept of the mentor and protégé is inspiring, but the reality is that it's a bit of a fairy tale for most of us.

Therefore, you need to find mentors yourself by seeking out people from whom you can learn. A mentor could be a more seasoned worker at the end of their career, a current high-flying superior who you work closely with, or an elder in your family. The more people you learn from, the better, as each viewpoint will impart a unique lesson. These people might not know it, but they will become your mentors, even if they aren't officially labelled as such.

The people we often look up to and learn from the most in our careers are our managers. Whether in sports or in an office, managers have a level of experience and expertise we do not. Additionally, a manager should lead by example, and you need to have a good manager, probably several good managers, who can teach you how to succeed in your work. Identifying those with much to offer and a willingness to work with you is an important skill that you must harness to benefit from their mentorship.

How do I climb through the ranks after passing probation?

Probation periods have been some of the most rewarding and challenging periods of my life, and getting out of probation in some jobs has meant the world to me. The sense of achievement was immense, even if my pay did not reflect that of a high achiever. Take a moment to give yourself a pat on the back for passing your probation. This is one of your career successes!

Now that you're a fully-fledged member of the team, you'll be looking at what comes next and how to make real progress in your career. What you need to demonstrate is consistency, dependability and loyalty, especially because you know that one day your motivation could wane, and you'll need other strengths to progress from one milestone to the next.

So, with your probation or interning days behind you, you want to establish yourself fully in your work. This next period of time is not only about developing your skills but also growing relationships with your colleagues. Most jobs require cross-team collaboration, and this is the perfect opportunity to become known in your job and build rapport across departments. Your manager will have been in your shoes and will understand who you need to meet and in which teams.

Therefore, you should ask your manager for those introductions to learn the key people and what they do. Ask for the core people who helped your manager over the years in each team. These are the people you want to form allegiances with. Go for drinks after work with them. Attend work social events, even if you don't normally enjoy socialising. It's an investment worth making. You don't need to kiss their asses. Just be nice, get to know them a little and let the relationships develop organically over time. By establishing those relationships, you are laying the foundations towards building unity between you and your colleagues.

While your relationships with other people at work will be fundamental toward helping your career development, don't forget to develop the single most important relationship of all: your relationship with yourself.

KEY TAKEAWAYS:

Starting a new job can be nerve-inducing, exciting and overwhelming. Getting through this period will depend largely on your attitude, your approach to probation (if applicable), how you develop your relationships with colleagues and how you manage your motivation. Below are some of the key takeaways from this chapter:

- Your attitude is vital. In the early stages of your career, focus on becoming better at what you do rather than making money
- Probation is about survival. Focus your efforts on demonstrating that you meet or exceed the standards required to become a valued member of the team
- Be kind and build rapport with colleagues, but accept that your job is not a popularity contest
- Experience pays but takes time to establish. Allow yourself enough time to develop the experience you are seeking
- Feeling overwhelmed is common, as are mistakes. Both are OK and are rarely fatal when you are new – don't beat yourself up over them
- Identify the chip on *your* shoulder and use it to drive yourself towards your goals

- Motivation is the catalyst in your pursuit of goals, but it is often temporary. What will see you through to the end are dedication, consistency and commitment.

Chapter 5

Feeling the Fear and Doing It Anyway

One of my mentors once said to me that while we all hope for long and successful careers, it's important to enjoy the journey. In hindsight those words are incredibly true. The small gains you make along the way should fill you with pride and act as a reminder that not only are you making the progress needed to become successful, but that you already *are* demonstrating success. If you don't enjoy the journey and the process, you are effectively wishing your life away for some future utopia that you may never reach. While progress will arrive in different shapes and forms, nothing is more rewarding than defeating the biggest obstacle of all – the person looking back at you in the mirror. *That* person is going to be your biggest foe, but you need to find a way to make them your best ally. In this chapter we will take a deeper dive into mindset. We'll look at personal growth, self-doubt, challenging your fears and some of the key emotional qualities you will need to confront to achieve mastery over your career mindset.

Isn't fear warning me to avoid harmful situations?

'The cave you fear to enter holds the treasure you seek.'

Joseph Campbell

Your career journey is going to be full of scary moments. Our first instinct when faced with fear is to run away because of the associated feelings of pain and risk. But the more you begin to understand fear, the more you will realise the sensation of fear could be your cue to act.

You will experience incidents during your career, good and bad, that help you learn how to manage certain situations. This is extremely important as learning how to deal with different situations is a part of what employers call 'experience'! This is not the only feedback your superiors will be looking out for, however. You'll need to demonstrate personal growth, not only for the benefit of your management team but, and perhaps more importantly, to enable the development of your own confidence and self-worth. Personal growth is where you gain mental strength, resilience and confidence.

What is personal growth?

Personal growth happens when you operate outside of your comfort zone, and your limits are tested and pushed. When you lift weights, for instance, your muscles are forced to adapt to the new strain, and the outcome is muscle growth. In many ways the mind works like the rest of the body, and if you are like me, then you are more convinced by theories if they can be backed by science.* Your mind – and your mental strength – will adapt as you exercise it further. New neural pathways are created when your mind is challenged and forced to cope with different scenarios. Memory cells will form, and your brain will create mechanisms for dealing with newly encountered situations that repeat themselves later. Lifting heavy weights hurts. But eventually, your muscle growth means that the pain becomes manageable, and you can lift heavier weights than before. By operating outside your comfort zone – by being *uncomfortable* – you are forcing yourself to adapt to ensure comfort in the future. This is personal growth.

How can I make personal growth happen to me?

'If you always do what you've always done,
you'll always get what you've always got.'
Henry Ford

Applying this quote to your career, it is only by pushing your boundaries that you will expose yourself to new things, and therein lies your growth potential. People don't like change or operating outside of their comfort zone because it can cause pain – both physical and psychological. However, you must push

* A good read on the science behind influence and persuasion can be found in Robert B. Cialdini's book *Influence: Science and Practice.*

yourself outside of your comfort zone to grow. Try something different. You need to believe that you can achieve your goals; otherwise, you won't do what is necessary to go after them. Once you start pushing yourself beyond your comfort ceiling, you'll see the real evidence of your personal growth and begin to wonder what other amazing things you can accomplish. You'll start to believe in yourself!

In writing this book I had an uncomfortable, albeit brief, realisation that in doing so, I was exposing myself to the world. Self-doubt crept in and told me to consider what people would think of me. Then, when travelling through airports and browsing the shelves of bookshops, I realised that many millions of people write books and, therefore, expose their minds to others. I don't think any less of them for doing so. In fact, I'm grateful for the value their stories and words add to my life. So if they can do that for me, why can't I do the same for others? Growth, success and achievement require you to make yourself vulnerable and demonstrate tenacity.

Why do I doubt myself so often?

In order to grow as a person, you need to move out of your own way. A fascinating aspect of human psychology is the inclination to self-sabotage. This stems from various factors such as a lack of self-esteem, negative self-talk, perfectionism and imposter syndrome, to name a few. To get out of your own way, you need to undergo a deep internal review of what happens in your mind when you doubt yourself. Very often, you are imagining false and negative scenarios about something that your brain interprets to be real. Then, because of this fear, you walk away. You need to develop the ability to identify self-doubt to distinguish perceived threats from real ones. When you understand that the threat is imaginary, you can choose to ignore it and move forward in spite of any alarm bells your mind might be signalling.

Knowing what self-doubt is and why it appears will not stop it from happening. However, your ability to label it as such will enable you to quickly identify when it happens and bash it on the head. Think of the arcade game Whack'A'Mole we all played as children. In life, you will need to play the mental version of this game all the time to bash down thoughts that don't serve you. Self-doubt Whack'A'Mole is a game we're all forced to play repeatedly in life. See a mole? Bash it!

Is bashing self-doubt easier said than done?

Bashing self-doubt is challenging, so this is where your tenacity enters the scene. Tenacity is undervalued and over-ridiculed, but what is tenacity? A dictionary search returns the following:

Courage, mettle, spirit, resolution
Strength to resist opposition, danger or hardship

In short, tenacity is the ability to demonstrate bravery.

What factors prevent us from being tenacious? Fear of ridicule, rejection and failure. Fear of being a laughingstock. Self-doubt and the thought, *'I am not good enough to do this.'* Remember, if you stay inside your comfort zone, you're not going to make it.

So what's it to be? Don't you want to be successful? You know you do. You *are* good enough. You just haven't put yourself through the adaptation process yet to understand what is going on beneath the surface. The sooner you start this process, the quicker your fears will begin to unravel.

Be vulnerable. Often, the things that scare you are nowhere near as bad as your worst fears. Instead of failing, you survive, and so you realise that you'll probably survive the next time, too. And the time after that. Eventually you'll figure out not only how to survive but also use that survival to thrive. Feel the fear and do it anyway. Once you get used to being vulnerable, a snowball effect occurs, and you become desensitised to your fears. Your skin grows a little thicker, and you realise you've cracked the code on how to grow and gain confidence. If you don't have the initial tenacity to put yourself out there, the journey can never begin. It's beautiful and totally worth it.

Who else should I take advice from?

As Theodore Roosevelt put it, *'It is not the critic who counts; not the man who points out how the strong man stumbles, or where the doer of deeds could have done them better. The credit belongs to the man who is actually in the arena, whose face is marred by dust and sweat and blood; who strives valiantly; who errs, who comes short again and again, because there is no effort without error and shortcoming; but who does actually strive to do the deeds; who knows great enthusiasms, the great devotions; who spends himself in a worthy cause; who at the best knows in the end the triumph of high achievement, and who at the worst, if he fails, at least fails while daring greatly, so that his place shall never be with those cold and timid souls who neither know victory nor defeat.'*

Take advice only from those already in the arena.

One of my managers referred to work as a battlefield that our team fought together on. I liked this analogy a lot, not only because of the sense of camaraderie and team spirit it generated but also because of the motivational aspect of fighting it out each day on the battleground. Get yourself down to the arena and take the hits.

As children we learn from our elders. We are taught not to touch wall sockets and not to cross the road without looking both ways. To stay away from high-up windows and to be careful about talking to strangers. We learn from those who know better than we do. It's important to remember this when deciding whose advice to take about your work and career goals. Our elders teach us general lessons in life about safety and survival. In work, it's a little more niche. Here, we want advice from those who either fight on our battleground or who used to do so.

That means current managers, senior team members, people who used to work in your job or field of career, or academics or trainers with that expertise. Why would you take advice from anybody who hasn't been there themselves? What value will that bring you?

Of course, it's up to you to decide those worthy of listening to. I've taken advice from people who worked in impressive careers but in totally different industries to the ones I've worked in. The lessons were more generalised but nonetheless highly valuable.

What I'm trying to say is be careful *not* to take advice from those without genuine and useful, relatable experience. If you're tenacious, you'll find there will always be people who try to talk you out of what you're doing. That is not the advice you're looking for, and more often than not, those people are not trying to help you. They want you to fail because your drive, motivation, tenacity and boldness simply highlight to them their own shortcomings. Your subsequent success will be a painful reminder to them of their own fears, failures and lack of drive. These people don't know better than you, and listening to them will not serve you positively in any way.

How do I know when to speak up at work?

I have been in company meetings where a superior will pose a question that nobody wants to answer in front of colleagues. The ensuing silence is painful. It's like fingernails screeching down a blackboard. All too often, people go into hiding during key meetings because they lack tenacity. It's not that they lack anything useful to add. They often do have valuable information they could contribute. It's that they lack the tenacity to speak up when the moment arrives. They are scared of what other people will think, and they doubt themselves. Eventually the braver ones answer the question with something that may or may not be helpful. Often, they will give an answer that you yourself had on the tip of your tongue. In this case, you missed an opportunity to demonstrate your value because you didn't speak up when the moment called for it.

Stop worrying about what other people think of you. If you're the kind of person who does so, the chances are you're a caring person in general, and those people you worry will think less of you will probably really like you for being nice anyway.

Part of making yourself vulnerable – and being tenacious – is refusing to hide and not being afraid to speak up. Offer contributions that are smart and make sense, and don't be afraid to ask questions. There is a common phrase in the workplace that there are no stupid questions. Sometimes, I preface a question with, 'Sorry if this is a stupid question, but…' as it completely disarms the narrative that the question is stupid if indeed it is.

One caveat, though. If you have nothing valuable to add, it is better to bite your tongue than to say something for the sake of it. Doing so could be counterproductive as people might not take you seriously in future and will view it as you trying to make yourself known. It will annoy your colleagues. It's OK to speak your mind or to let people know your thoughts on a predicament or question, but try to ensure your words add value.

How should I respond to setbacks?

Setbacks, whether fleeting or persistent, come in a variety of different shapes and degrees of severity. However, they can all be managed and overcome. Successfully navigating setbacks not only diminishes self-doubt but also reinforces your ability to tackle challenges. As a result, future obstacles seem less like problems and more like learning opportunities. Let's use a scientific analogy to illustrate this point below.

The common cold can be unpleasant. When a virus invades the cells in our nose and throat, it replicates and destroys them. Our body's defence starts with white blood cells called macrophages, which identify and consume these virus invaders. If the viral load becomes too high, causing the virus to replicate faster than it's being destroyed, then eventually, the virus will win out over the macrophages, leading to inflammation, a sore throat, and congested sinuses. The battle is lost, and a setback is encountered. But the war is far from over.

A new battalion of troops is deployed – B-cells and T-cells. B-cells create antibodies specific to the virus and mark them for the T-cells, which then target and destroy them altogether. The war is won, and you begin to feel better.

After the dust has settled, a few of those B and T-cells remain in the blood and retain the memory of the defeated virus so that if or when you encounter that particular foe again, those cells will remember the invader and will reactivate and replicate, enabling a swift victory at the next encounter.

This ability to overcome setbacks is innate. Be it a mistake at work, not securing a hoped-for bonus or facing a layoff, the key is to rise again. Only this time, you'll be better prepared to strategise for the results you want.

I'll discuss the nature of setbacks in more detail in a later chapter.

Should I be worried about performance reviews?

Performance reviews, an appraisal by superiors and/or colleagues, gauge how well you're performing at work. They can be periodic, or you might need to proactively ask your manager for one. Performance reviews can seem scary – this is one of those instances where your fear of failure and self-doubt can bubble to the surface as your flaws will be highlighted and exposed. How does that sound? Uncomfortable?

Here's the thing. Performance reviews matter. A lot. If you want to get better at what you do, you need to know what you're not doing well enough first. You need that constructive criticism to develop and improve your skills.

However, performance reviews require delicate honesty by those providing your feedback. You need to have the emotional maturity to understand that even though the feedback might be exposing your weaknesses, the review is informing you about which areas of your performance you need to attack and enhance to become a better version of yourself.

Good, honest performance reviews are priceless. Embrace them. Rather than taking feedback personally, accept the improvement challenge that has been set for you and commit to tackling it.

How can I set goals for my career?

Identify senior roles that inspire, excite or interest you if you plan to stay with your employer for the long term. This will inform the knowledge you'll need to acquire, the acquaintances you need to develop and the skills you will need to demonstrate, which will help you understand your purpose and the direction you need to take at work. If your goals cannot be met by your current employer, identifying senior roles will help you understand where the end of the road is at your current workplace so you can plan what the next chapter looks like for you. These steps will inform your high-level career strategy, but it is helpful to break it down further into baby steps that you can accomplish on a quarterly, bi-annual or yearly basis.*

How important is data in decision-making?

In the new age of technology and AI, data should be used where possible in everything you do. A former colleague of mine – a data engineer – once told me that data helps people make informed decisions. Moreover, data provides statistical analysis of things such as how you compare to competitors, how your company revenue has changed, where gains and losses stem from

* One protocol for setting career and company goals is the OKR (Objectives and Key Results) methodology with further reading to be found in the book *Measure What Matters* by John Doerr.

and, therefore, how to rectify them. It will inform you about factors such as average earnings made in your job category so you can assess whether your compensation is fair. And it will also tell you how your industry is faring and how others compare. Data underpins huge decision-making processes at the highest level and provides people with an analytical edge that did not previously exist. Data can also help you analyse your own performance.

Today, many if not most employers use data analytics tools for feedback about performance, progress and comparisons with competitors. One of the first things I ask for when starting a new job is how I can gain access to these tools. By doing so, it means I can seek out areas of weakness that can be worked on. Presenting this feedback to colleagues and superiors demonstrates that you are taking initiative and not waiting for performance reviews to be told where improvements may be required.

Use data where you can to give yourself an advantage in your work and in your life. It will help you make assessments around risk, probabilities and the strategic direction you should take.

When will I know when I've realised my career goals?

As you progress throughout your career, there will be times when you feel like you know everything there is to know about your job. This is dangerous because it is both a blessing and a curse. At first, it will feel good to excel, and managers will be happy with you and your performance. All is good, and the growing pains you had to endure to get there are over. Everything is comfortable. You are satisfied.

However, danger begins to seep in in the form of complacency. There is merit to consistent performance at your level for a time, but eventually, if you're not learning something new, then you're beginning to stagnate. Stagnation is laziness' ugly sibling, and you risk becoming unsatisfied and losing your drive. We seem to always want more than what we have. This is not to negate the practices of humility and gratitude, but rather that if you have higher goals than those you have already accomplished in your career, you're going to need to do something to make them happen. Nothing will come to you unless you're prepared to potentially wait a very long time. On more than one occasion I've seen the career progression of a person borne out of the resignation or retirement of another. Are you really OK with hanging around for that to happen? We'll discuss achieving promotions in further detail later; however, I want to begin our thinking about this dilemma now.

If a promotion is not on the horizon, take consistent baby steps until it is. Be curious. Ideally, you are in your job because this curiosity is inherently within you regardless. Try to learn one new thing every day about your job, company or industry, even if it's something really small. This is not a difficult task, but by doing so, you will constantly grow and improve, adding little nuggets of wisdom on your way to mastery and expertise.

KEY TAKEAWAYS:

In this chapter we looked at career mindset a little deeper and considered how this interacts with career progression. We also explored how fear manifests and the best ways to deal with this. Below are some more key takeaways from this chapter:

- Personal growth happens when you feel discomfort but continue regardless
- You should confront self-sabotage by bashing self-doubt on the head
- Tenacity will push you out of your comfort zone and lead to growth
- Don't allow fear to hold you back from demonstrating your value to others
- Setbacks are a part of life and are an opportunity to understand failure and how to overcome it
- Seek out constructive performance reviews so you can understand where you need to improve
- Discover how you can use data to your (and your employer's) advantage
- Stagnation is a threat to your drive and job satisfaction – keep moving forward, even if slowly

Chapter 6

Preventing Burnout

I heard of burnout in my younger adult life but presumed it was rare and associated with a severe breakdown of some sort. I read about warnings of not overdoing it or pushing too hard and burning out. Since then, I have experienced burnout myself, and when talking to somebody else recently who also experienced it, I realised our burnouts manifested entirely differently. Nevertheless, both were significantly responsible for us deciding to call time on our jobs. I have also witnessed and spoken to several other colleagues and acquaintances who have experienced burnout. It turns out that burnout is not that uncommon at all. As burnout is real and surprisingly common, this chapter looks at what burnout is, why it happens and what you can do to prevent it from happening in your career.

What is burnout?

Some folks described their burnout manifesting as a feeling of nausea and that they were physically gagging before leaving home to go to work every day. The mere thought of leaving the house to go to work caused a crippling and overwhelming dread. Others have found that the levels of stress they needed to endure induced severe anxiety, meaning they needed to take medical leave to reset.

For me, I found I had lost a lot of desire and will to persist. My motivation had completely dissipated, and along with it, the commitment and dedication I had previously demonstrated in that same job. I had spent two years in quite possibly my favourite job ever. But it was very intense from day one. By the end, my patience was wiped out completely because it felt like things had changed at the company beyond repair. I realised I had begun to lash out at people in meetings, and this sent alarm bells ringing because that was completely uncharacteristic of me. Something wasn't working anymore, and it was a signal to me that it was time to step away.

Burnout is best described as reaching a point of either physical or emotional exhaustion. This exhaustion can encompass your energy levels, motivation, happiness and your will to endure. Looking at the description provided by the charity Mental Health UK, other common signs of burnout include *feeling tired or drained most of the time, feeling helpless or trapped, feeling detached or alone, having a cynical outlook, self-doubt, procrastination and feeling overwhelmed.*

My goal is to work on things I find fun. If the fun is not there, it will likely spell trouble. I realised that many of the symptoms of burnout described above were there in some form during the time I experienced it. But most importantly to me, the fun wasn't there anymore in my job. So I stepped away and took a few months out to recharge my batteries before trying again at a different job. The key here was to recognise that I had burned out and to act on it. If *you* reach this point and realise your job is the root cause and not some other situation in your life, you have to do something about it. Take some time off work, whether that's using your holiday allowance or stepping away entirely if you can afford to do so.* Failing that, it's probably time to look for something new. It can be very damaging to continue working in an environment that causes burnout. There are many people I have worked with whose work environments became untenable due to burnout, and they all did something to change their scenarios for the better.

Some company work cultures are more likely to lead to burnout because they are inherently intense places to work. It's not always possible to avoid this, but there are certain things that you can do and some principles to adhere to in your work style and structure to minimise and mitigate the risk of burnout.

How can I adjust my working style to avoid burnout?

I like the process of working in sprints. The concept of working in sprints is derived from the "Agile" methodology of project

---

* If you can, try to save as you earn. If you have a six-month (change this amount as you see fit) buffer to cover your costs and expenses while out of work, it will enable you to step away from damaging work environments so that you can reconfigure and make your next career move objectively.

management and involves intense periods of work to deliver a given project or task and then reducing the pace before the next sprint begins. During sprints, days can be long and extremely busy. You might get to 4 p.m. and realise you haven't eaten anything that day. During the period between sprints, you can catch up on the lower-priority items on your task list that require less intense focus.

In Agile methodology, a sprint is a defined period of one or two weeks in which a team 'scrums' together to complete a task list. It is commonly used by technology companies, but its principles can be adapted to fit many different types of work.

I find intense periods of work thrilling, exciting and rewarding. Quiet and dull days at work are boring and make a day last an age. When working in sprints, I feel like I'm working with purpose and making progress. However, sprints are not for everybody. Others may prefer a middle ground with a more consistent intensity. Find a pace that is suitable for you and the work you're doing. It's really important to do what works best for you. Some cars are high-octane and sporty; others aren't as fast but burn through fuel more slowly. We are all built differently. Don't force yourself past your limits, whatever those are. This, of course, is not a licence to slack. Your limits might be different to others, but you should still aim to push yourself as much as you can handle and deliver your work to a high standard. If you're delivering in your work, don't compare yourself to others. You can defend your work ethic with your results.

Sprints sound very intense. Is it sustainable?

It is imperative that you find the time to disconnect and unplug. Taking time away often means using holiday allowance, but it could also refer to periods of time off between jobs. I find that I need one week off per quarter to disconnect and recharge my batteries. Again, it depends on what the job is and what you yourself need. The key here is to disconnect mentally as much as possible and re-energise yourself as required. Sometimes, the intensity of consistent work can make you mentally jaded. A time-out can serve as a mental and physical reboot. An exhausted employee won't perform to a high standard. It's no good for you or your employer if you burn out. So take a deserved break.

Finally, while a physical time out for a week or longer will help recharge your batteries, it's important to disconnect in smaller portions throughout the year. Whether that's relaxing during evenings and weekends or partaking in other useful practices like meditation, exercise and socialising.

What practices should I be considering in my personal time?

There are several useful things you can be doing to offset the risk of burning out.

Meditation and Mindfulness

I used to think that meditation was for hippies. I imagined a group of people sitting in the woods in a circle humming in unison and thought, 'that's not me.' In one job, a colleague of mine introduced me to the idea of meditating on the train to and from work. He said it worked for him because he could close his eyes, and it looked like he was taking a nap to the rest of the train – much like other passengers do anyway. However, he was using that time each morning and night to look after his mind. I decided to try it. 'What's the worst that could happen?' I thought. I meditated consistently for a few weeks, and eventually, it became part of my daily routine. Headphones on, eyes closed, and the rest of the world was blanked out.

There are different types of meditation, so please investigate this topic further and discover what works best for you. I liked mindfulness meditation most as it combines breathing exercises with the observance of body and thought. Mindfulness helped me to understand my mind a little better and how to manage the hundreds of thoughts that appear every day. At the very least, breathing exercises flood the body with oxygen, the life force of all living beings, which also induces a feeling of calm and tranquillity. What's not to like about that?

TRY IT NOW:

Since you're reading this book, I know you have a moment to try something out. So, before turning over to the next page, do this for me:

Close your eyes. Take a deep breath. Inhale for four seconds, hold for four seconds, then exhale for four seconds.

Wait four seconds after fully exhaling, then repeat a further three times.

You will likely notice a difference in how you feel after taking just three or four deep breaths. Now imagine how it feels to do this for ten, twenty or thirty minutes per day over consecutive days, weeks and months.

Like all exercise, the results take time – perhaps a couple of weeks or more. To notice the benefits requires consistency and patience. Eventually, you will harvest from your efforts an ability to separate your thoughts from reality to induce a state of calmness. Meditation became a very helpful tool for me to manage difficult situations in all aspects of life, as well as the ability to withstand stress and reduce the risk of burnout. Even ten minutes a day makes a difference.

I particularly like the guided meditations on the "Insight Timer" app, which you can download for free on smartphone app stores. Apple watches also have an in-built mindfulness feature that prompts you to carry out breathing exercises when it recognises an increase in your heart rate. Access to meditation tools has never been easier, so be sure to give it a go.

Exercise

Exercise causes the body to release feel-good chemicals into the bloodstream. It additionally makes your body fitter and more able to withstand stress. It's no wonder that exercise is recommended for everybody.

Find an exercise that works for you. If your knees are worn out from playing sports in your earlier years, there's no point in taking up running. Some advice indicates a combination of resistance training (like lifting weights) and cardio is beneficial for several reasons. Again, don't overdo it, or you'll risk physical burnout.

Human evolution did not involve spending hours per day hunched over a keyboard at a desk. Our bodies need physical activity. Whatever it is, whether brisk walking or a gym routine, get up and move every day.

Diet

Try to limit your sugar intake. Sugar is a quick fix. You'll crash shortly after consuming it and crave more. It'll also make you gain weight, making exercise more cumbersome. If you find yourself reaching for sugary foods often, it could be a sign that you're not getting enough sleep or rest. You should additionally ensure that you stay hydrated. Even a small drop in hydration levels has been proven to affect concentration.* Caffeine has been shown to be

---

*https://www.ncbi.nlm.nih.gov/pmc/articles/PMC4207053/#:~:text=Problems%20with%20cognitive%20performance%20that,anxiety%20(4%2C21).

relatively safe in moderate quantities and helps many people stay alert and focused. However, it is also a diuretic, meaning it causes you to lose water, so stay hydrated if you consume caffeine. Excessive caffeine can also make people feel nervous, anxious and affect sleep quality, so be mindful of your tolerance to it. It goes without saying that excessive alcohol consumption and smoking should be avoided.

Sleep

The average adult needs somewhere between seven to nine hours of sleep per night. If you consistently sleep less than this, ensure you don't consume caffeine too late in the day, as it might be keeping you awake. Consistently getting less than seven hours of sleep will mean you eventually build up a sleep deficit, leading to the risk of chronic fatigue and, you guessed it, burnout. If you don't already, then try to get at least seven hours per night and adjust from there if you feel like it's not enough.

How will my personal life affect my career?

I have already written about bringing the best version of yourself into work. So, in this section, I'll focus more on romance and family. Spending many hours per day and several days per week at work with people can generate romantic interest. From what

I've seen, it often ends badly when romantic relationships are forged between colleagues. There are one or two examples of office romances culminating in marriage, but more often than not, the relationships don't work out. As the saying goes, there are plenty of fish in the sea, so it would be prudent to keep your romantic life outside of the workplace. Otherwise, you are inviting distraction or worse into your working environment, and this will harm your productivity and potentially your reputation, too. Adding an additional layer of stress (good or bad) to your work environment can also contribute to burnout.

In their personal lives, some people decide to start families. I used to worry that family commitments would be a threat to my career ambitions. You can understand why some people choose to avoid or delay having a family because it enables them to focus solely on their career and remove financial and emotional obligations towards other people. However, as my career progressed, I realised that many of my CEOs, senior executives and colleagues were parents to young children. I thought to myself that if these people manage it with their considerable working obligations and responsibilities, then it must be feasible. Companies and local laws are quite generous towards new parents these days, with many offering maternal and/or paternal benefits. When I became a father, I enjoyed some of the most successful and rewarding years of my career and personal life. So my conclusion is that family avoidance for career gains can be a bit of a myth. What I will add, however, is that starting a family will change your financial commitments. So, to a certain extent, it's about timing it correctly and having a supportive environment around you that can enable both work and personal enrichment concurrently. The decision around having a family is very much unique to the individual, and there is no right or wrong answer here. Do what works for you.

What about socialising at work?

Earlier I mentioned not showing up to work hungover when trying to make a good impression. While you should ideally never show up to work hungover, some of the best connections I've made with people over the years, including with clients, were over a beer. I've also seen many people embarrass themselves because they have a low alcohol tolerance. Some lost their jobs because of how they behaved under the influence of alcohol when socialising with work colleagues. There is certainly a difference between bad personal habits and social development in a career context; you just need to ensure you find a balance. Too much socialising could mean you're not getting enough downtime to stay energised at work.

What other things can you do to stay healthy and prevent burnout?

Spend time consuming self-development and self-improvement material like you are currently by reading this book. I used to read on the train while commuting to or from work to pass the time productively alongside my meditation. Mental health and self-help are no longer taboo topics, so don't be embarrassed about being seen reading books on these topics in public.

The power of positive thinking

What is positive thinking? There is a wealth of literature out there on this subject. Simply search for the 'law of attraction' online, and you'll find endless material – with a book called *The Secret* probably being the most publicised. The premise of positive thinking revolves around transmitting positive thoughts into the universe and envisioning your desired future. *'Ask, believe, receive.'*

There's no witchcraft or magic at play here (or is there . . .?). Positive, upbeat and can-do thinking may well affect the uplifting chemicals produced in the brain, making you more motivated and energised. And this energy gets noticed by other people. Hiring managers I've spoken to have always highlighted the concept of a 'can-do' attitude as highly desirable in candidates. People will be drawn to you and will feed off your vibrancy. Such people may include not only hiring managers but also those who nominate other employees (like you) for promotion, clients and people you pitch or present to. Think about some of the most inspiring, bubbly and energetic personalities you've seen in people. Doesn't being around them make you feel more motivated and positive yourself? The effect these people have on others can be described as magic because they are able to transform the moods of others. Whether or not you believe there is a supernatural element to it, by thinking positively, you are drawing the right kind of attention and associated opportunities to yourself.

This mentality also buys you credit if you need to take some downtime or if you're having a bad day or week. People are more likely to cut you some slack and write off a blip in performance if they know that's not the real you.

KEY TAKEAWAYS:

One of the most important things you can do to give yourself the best chance of career success and progress is to look after yourself so you are able to perform at work. We've talked about preventing burnout and the ways to mitigate and prevent it. Additionally, we've discussed:

- Understanding the signs of burnout. Be sure to make changes if you begin to experience them, including assessing whether you should continue in your job
- Taking steps to pre-empt and manage burnout by adapting your working pace to produce results while maintaining a healthy lifestyle
- Following the core aspects of a healthy lifestyle, including a healthy mind, a good diet, exercise, rest and good sleep
- Pursuing personal relationships that are conducive to high performance at work
- Balancing socialisation at work, as socialisation can be either good or bad
- The power of positive thinking on yourself and those around you

Chapter 7

Managing Competition and Standing Out from the Crowd

Competition is something we must all deal with in one way or another throughout our lives. Some people are highly competitive by nature, and others are less so. Wherever you stand on the spectrum of competition, it is something you will have to confront and manage at various stages of your career. Therefore, this chapter takes a closer look at the origins of competition, why it's important, how you should respond to it and use it to further your career and the importance of emotional maturity.

What are the origins of competition?

Competitive tendencies are a natural result of human evolution. Living organisms have been competing for limited resources for centuries – whether that be food, mating partners or living space. Our instinct to survive and reproduce has engrained competitiveness into our DNA. Today, our ingrained competitiveness still creates a resolve to eat, reproduce and reside in suitable habitats, but humans have established a relatively civilised society whereby the fight is not as fierce as it might once have been. Nonetheless, competition spills into several domains, such as school, sports, geopolitics, industry and business, which in turn trickles down into the workplace.

Why is competition important?

In sports, for example, a team depends on other competitors to, at the very least, make up the numbers required to facilitate the competition itself. If all teams in a sporting competition went out of business except for one, the whole competition would fail because that team has no opponents to compete against. In business, competition is protected by law to ensure consumers receive better prices, as well as for job creation and to encourage innovation. Competition laws manufacture an environment that facilitates and encourages competition for the betterment of society.

But what about competition in the workplace, where you will compete with others, initially to win an offer of employment and then to keep and excel in your job? In this setting, competition is essential, and you will need to learn how to embrace it and succeed in spite of it. Competition presents a fabulous opportunity to learn from those who have progressed further than you and to stand out from the crowd. This is especially possible if you are able to be your authentic, positive self when others are less capable.

Some of the folks I've worked with (and competed against) have been tasked with achieving the same targets as me, and we would ultimately be judged and compared by how we fared against one another. A scenario such as this creates a pressure that keeps you on your toes and harnesses a sense of urgency. It motivates you to push yourself to your limits and to travel outside of your comfort zone and into the growth zone.

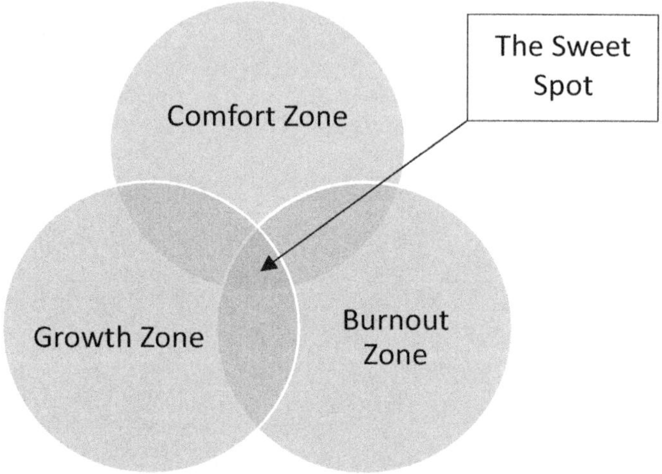

Some of the people I've 'competed' with became amazing friends and acquaintances. We had the best times together even though we were competing to be the number one person in our jobs. There comes a time when you learn to respect other warriors fighting on the same battleground as you. This can be observed among athletes all the time. The battles they have with each other can turn very nasty, even violent. It doesn't look like they are friends because they're technically enemies during periods of competition. But when the competition is over, they hug, embrace and congratulate each other. This is the beauty of competition, and it extends to all forms of work. And the more scars each warrior bears from the battlefield, the more respect is given and gained.

<u>How does competition make you feel?</u>

Adrenaline is a chemical more commonly referred to as the 'fight or flight' hormone. We all know what adrenaline feels like. Sudden stress causes your body to release a shot of adrenaline into your bloodstream. Your heart starts beating really fast, and your breathing gets heavier, forcing oxygenated blood to your muscles and organs quickly in case you need to react to an imminent threat. Your pupils dilate, and your brain moves into its highest state of alertness. Your body is in its best condition to fight or escape an attack. Adrenaline is another evolutionary trait that was required for us to stave off injury or death and to survive.

Cortisol, also known as the stress hormone, is another chemical that is released when in a state of fight or flight. Cortisol increases the sugar in your bloodstream to help provide energy to your cells and to fuel your body in case it needs to act.

When we are competing we are, in a way, fighting. It may not be a physical battle, but our brains don't know any other way to interpret this threat. If you're fighting to be the number one graphic designer at a company, or for a job that is interviewing a hundred other candidates, or for a promotion or pay rise only available to a select few, it can activate the exact same sensory receptors. The body reacts how it always has done when fighting – by releasing these hormones. However, too much of these hormones can be a bad thing. Fatigue, anxiety, weight gain, increased blood pressure and headaches are all possible consequences of cortisol and adrenaline when released in excess. These symptoms are damaging for both the body and mind if experienced over a long time. This is why you need to be at the top of your mental game and take steps to prevent burnout to mitigate, if not nullify, the risk of long-term harm.

What about people who take competition too far?

Everywhere you work there will always be one person, or several people, who have a prickly temperament, who will cheat or who are straight-up nasty. You can't leave one job for another, hoping to never encounter unpleasant people at work again. I'm sorry to disappoint you, but you will need to work with incompetent, annoying and nasty people in every line of work. In every cross-section of society, you will encounter the good, the bad and the ugly. All these people end up in work, regardless of the industry. This means that the bad eggs need to be dealt with rather than avoided. There will be times when you need to stand up for yourself or have the mental strength to not let these people get to you

Granted, you could have a boss from hell, and it's worth getting away from seriously bad actors that make your work environment too toxic. You need to figure out your line in the sand and ensure you do not cross it to keep your adrenaline and cortisol levels healthy. But do make sure you ask yourself whether you're using a difficult boss or colleague as a scapegoat for your lack of application.

The best way to deal with difficult colleagues is to put your best foot forward. Be the best version of yourself and have the patience to allow whatever time needs to pass for the cream (that's you!) to rise to the top.

What mentality should I have when working with nasty people?

You're going to have some bad days. It's inevitable. Someone might get one over you, or you might feel that you've been 'stabbed in the back' in some way. Workplaces are often very political environments, even if they outwardly state that toxicity is not tolerated. You may find yourself on the receiving end of nasty politics on multiple occasions. This could come in the form of undue criticisms, stitch-ups to make you accountable for the failures of someone else or others claiming ownership of your good work and ideas. When this happens, remember why it happened and what you can do to prevent it from happening again. Don't worry about losing battles along the way. Your career, your work and your life are a marathon, not a sprint.

If you work in something you enjoy or even love, then the competition is an inconvenience. It becomes something you have to overcome and be better than to encourage you to excel. If your competition wants to play dirty - let them. They are using tricks at your expense to mask their own flaws. Smart superiors can and do see through these illusions. Always ensure your good work is visible to your superiors so you gain the recognition you deserve. Silence your critics with your work, not your words.

How do I stand out from my competition?

'No pressure, no diamonds.'

Thomas Carlyle

The weight of pressure can turn things either into dust or diamonds. If you can prevent burnout, you can withstand or even enjoy pressure. Thriving under pressure is not something everyone you work with will be able to withstand. Combine this skill with your commitment, knowledge and application of your work, and this is where the fun really begins. Focus on consistent and dedicated application and it will show in the results you produce. Over time your consistency will illustrate that you are a dependable member of the team. Managers love to have team members that they can rely on and if you can brush off any negative encounters you experience with your competition through your consistent performance it will nullify any threat that they pose.

It's incredibly powerful to have mastery over both work and emotional maturity. At this stage of your development, you can truly be your authentic self, have fun and be creative. You have the wisdom you need to succeed and the skill that comes with your experience. This breeds the confidence to be tenacious while applying yourself correctly. When you are in this state of flow, you're glowing in your work; you can't be stopped, and it shows! You have achieved the perfect balance between your temperament and achieving the desired results in your job, and you'll stand out for it.

I find my ego gets in the way sometimes. How can I control it?

Dealing with your ego is difficult. The ego is a stubborn thing. It's ever-present and defines who we are. Or so it would have you believe. Your ego is your personal identity. From ego is derived a person's sense of self-esteem or self-importance. Ego can be proud, immature, childish and selfish. It craves control. It can influence your impulses and cause you to make mistakes, sometimes rash ones. It often does not have time for reason or measured control.

Understanding ego, both that you have one and how it works, is the only way to manage it. If you cannot manage your ego, you're not ready for the big time. You will lose control, make errors and impinge on any faith that superiors and decision-makers had about you.

Your competition will likely have a powerful ego that will challenge yours. You're both after a prize that either cannot be shared or, if it must be shared, of which the victor will keep the largest slice. How you deal with their ego and manage yours will greatly affect how you fare against them. Your ego will see you compare yourself against others, which can lead to self-doubt, overconfidence, fear, threat, envy and conflict.

Ego is a beast that must be tamed, or else it'll tame you.

When you're able to tame your ego, you can harness its strengths and gain awareness of its weaknesses while making decisions. You can consider whether a decision is 'just your ego talking', or whether it is driving you towards something important. Ego gives us our sense of purpose, pride and endeavour, which all breed confidence. Therefore, ego can be a good thing, too, so you need to develop the ability to step away and analyse whether it is serving you well in any given moment. The ability to do this demonstrates to others you have a level of emotional maturity that most others do not.

What is 'emotional maturity'?

Someone who has their ego in check demonstrates signs of emotional maturity. To make progress in your career and life, you must be able to stomach disappointment, criticism, let downs and failure. This means you need to have the ability to deal with other people, bad actors, critics and setbacks and not take it personally when things don't go your way. You need to be able to receive constructive feedback and criticism with grace. Your competition might currently be better than you, but rather than letting that demoralise and dishearten you, use it as motivation instead. You need to be able to stay calm in the face of chaos and unease and continue to show up on the battleground each day because you want to be there no matter what happens.

The ability to manage emotions is closely intertwined with mastery of ego. To be able to control both collectively portrays emotional maturity. And by having emotional maturity, you are demonstrating that you have leadership qualities.

How can I handle competition within a team?

'Being a team player' is a quality you will notice is asked for quite often in job advertisements. So, while it's important to focus on yourself and become your best version, you must also refine your ability to work in a team. You will often find that you need to demonstrate an ability to work both independently *and* with others in a team. When doing the latter, it is vital that you can control your competitive instincts and bring your individual qualities to the table for the benefit of the team.

American psychologist Bruce Tuckman proposed the concept of 'Forming, Storming, Norming and Performing' (FSNP) as the four stages of psychological development a team goes through when working on a project. Understanding these stages is crucial. It enables you to process what's happening when a team comes together and the different events that occur throughout the lifecycle of your project. Even if your work is not heavily project-based, you will be able to draw parallels to these stages when the composition of a team naturally changes over time due to the churn of personnel and different eras of a company's lifecycle.

During the 'Forming' stage, the team begins to address a problem and propose solutions. During the 'Storming' stage, roles are established and assigned to each person. This stage is considered the most dangerous because it can lead to turf wars and conflict. The less (bad) ego and toxicity here, the better because this is where the biggest risk of team collapse lies. 'Norming' is where everyone begins to buy into the process and develop trust and rapport with each other. 'Performing' is where the team starts to really excel because everyone has prioritised working together for the good of the common goal. If you notice these phases playing out with your colleagues when working together, you can even bring FSNP to their attention. This might help to reduce the risk of turf wars and ego-driven behaviour that could scupper the likelihood of success during the 'Storming' stage.

Tuckman later introduced an 'Adjourning' stage, which comes after the completion of the project or after targets have been met. Here, accomplishments are celebrated and rewarded, and depending on how successful the project was, the organisation might assign a new project or target to the same team.

KEY TAKEAWAYS:

This chapter was about competition. Hopefully you've learnt more about how it forms the basis of our evolution, why it is important and how you can use it to your advantage. To recap, we discussed the following:

- Competition is enshrined in human nature and society, and rather than shying away from it, you need to learn how to thrive in competitive working environments by embracing the growth zone
- The importance of understanding how competition makes you feel. If you are good at what you do, you will undoubtedly excel, regardless of what your competition is doing. Don't forget: the cream rises to the top
- Being good at something requires not only skill but also the ability to manage your ego. Learn to identify when your ego is serving you well and when it might hinder you
- Nothing demonstrates mastery over ego better than emotional maturity – you will get noticed for it if you portray it
- Don't let competition scupper your qualities as a team player

Chapter 8

Achieving Promotion

Promotion at work often entails some kind of leadership aspect, including taking on greater accountability, more difficult tasks than previously undertaken and responsibility over others in more junior positions. Nowadays there are even junior manager roles at companies, meaning leadership qualities are highly sought after by employers at all levels of the career hierarchy. Most, if not all, of us who are in a traditional job will find the reward of a promotion as something that drives us to push ourselves to be better at our jobs and work harder to prove our value. Therefore, this chapter looks at promotion. We will discuss the leadership qualities that will help you get promoted, what you need to prove to be considered for one, why simply working hard and delivering is sometimes not enough and the hidden challenges that promotions entail.

What are some distinguishing features commonly seen in leaders?

Leadership traits include great communication skills, the ability to help others improve, expertise, experience, confidence and trustworthiness. Leaders possess assertiveness, and at their very best lead by example. These are people who you can look up to and learn from. Great leaders can motivate their community or team and win their admiration. And when these required qualities are absent, the respect and trust we have for them is diminished, sometimes catastrophically.

Leaders are present at every level of the career hierarchy. Junior leadership, senior leadership and team leadership.* Some companies have specific leadership teams, and supplementary functions are created with the prime purpose of supporting the people identified as leaders at the company.

To prove your leadership credentials, you will need to demonstrate that you have the expertise, experience and emotional maturity to spearhead your group and guide and direct them on how to overcome their goals, targets and objectives (both collectively and individually). You will need to be able to manage different people with different personalities, and you will be expected to deal with any obstacles they are experiencing when trying to execute their work by fighting their battles for them, whether internally or externally. Moving into a leadership role means you are not only responsible for your own wellbeing but also that of others. If you think you're ready to be a leader, you need to consider all of the above and give an honest assessment of yourself. Then, decide whether you can rise to the challenges leaders face.

Some leaders are given responsibilities beyond their abilities. Often, these people were assigned to their position because their

---

* I recommend reading *The High Potential Leader* by Ram Charan for anyone looking to move into leadership roles at work.

former manager exited, and they slotted into the role by default. This means you will find people in leadership positions who lack the right qualities to execute them. It can be a nightmare to work with bad leaders because it can leave that business unit rudderless, demoralised and unable to achieve its growth potential.

What does it take to be a good leader?

Aside from possessing expertise, experience and emotional maturity, the best leaders lead by example. This doesn't necessarily mean they work like crazy all day and night – they might be very efficient and not need to. A good leader should be someone who has your back during conflict, someone who you trust and who empowers you. They need to be honest with you and inform you of what you are doing well and where you need to improve. Good leaders are respected by their peers and team members. They are calm, analytical and measured. They do not hide, and they make and commit to decision-making where others dither and avoid accountability. Leaders command respect because they possess special qualities that others lack. Common interpersonal qualities I've seen in great leaders include good humour, personal interest in team members' wellbeing, and being relatable on a human level. Fighting on the battleground with inspiring leaders makes work ever so much more enjoyable.

Leadership qualities aside, what else is needed for promotion?

In order to make a case for yourself as a candidate for promotion, you'll be expected to show real results and accomplishments in your work to date. You'll need to present any deliverables and be able to prove your track record. When meeting with your boss or a new employer, you should prepare evidence that demonstrates how you have made a positive contribution to your work. Turning up to work on time, being polite and respectful and generally displaying competency are a given. The decision maker will want to see quantifiable ways you have added value. What did you do that led to revenue growth at the company during your time there? How much revenue were you directly responsible for, if applicable? Did you help your company grow market share among your competition? By how much? What percentage? What products or services did you help launch? What projects did you help deliver on? What was your role in it? Are you able to replicate that success easily? What resources will you need to do so? What gaps in the market have you identified through your prior work that will help you bring an edge to your employer? Be ready and able to show why and how you will benefit the company.

How important is my network in all this?

I have been given jobs via all sorts of gateways, from applying for jobs on job sites to introductions to blindly sending out my CV using a 'hit and hope' strategy. However, I have come to realise that over time, my network is what has reaped the most reward for me. When I was younger, I heard about the importance of networking and thought this meant going to networking events and engaging in small talk. But in actuality, your professional network largely stems from the connections you make with people when *at* work. The reason that in-work connections are the strongest is because in working with people, you develop your rapport with them, and they get to see first-hand who you are and how you operate. You are a known entity rather than a name on a CV or LinkedIn profile. This means you can find work opportunities that completely circumvent an arduous application and interview process.

How can I grow my network?

'I've learned that people will forget what you said, people will forget what you did, but people will never forget how you made them feel.'

Maya Angelou.

If you make people smile, laugh and feel good about themselves, they will remember it. It may not be a conscious memory, but their subconscious mind will associate you with those positive feelings and joy. Making people feel great by connecting with them using your authentic best self is the secret to making lifelong connections with the people who will form your network. Your network is essentially the portfolio of contacts you have made during your career and life. Connect with people on a human level. Do not be fake. Cut out the crap. Be your genuine self; be enthusiastic, curious, kind and funny, and people will remember you for it. And those people will not only remember you for it, but they will want you in their lives. We spend most of our waking lives with work colleagues rather than friends or family. The people you make the best connections with will want to work with someone who they like and get along with. Grow and use your network.

How can I negotiate from a strong bargaining position?

Promotions can be awarded in several ways. A vacancy might be advertised internally, someone higher up the chain might leave or retire, or you might decide to change jobs to achieve a promotion your current employer cannot give you.

Negotiating a promotion or a new job and the associated benefits, including salary, bonuses and other incentives, can be done from either a position of strength or weakness. You want to be in a strong bargaining position when negotiating a promotion. The strongest bargaining position to be in is one where you are willing and able to walk away from the deal. You are more likely to get your preferred terms this way because there is usually a range of acceptable outcomes for both parties during a negotiation, and by being willing to walk away, your counterpart is more likely to be massaged into their least favourable but nevertheless acceptable final agreement.

If you're willing to walk away, you will be seen as a serious person and will seem more confident because you have other options on your plate, and you know that you are desirable to others who are more willing to offer you terms that you deem acceptable. It also portrays to the other party they are losing something of value by not matching what a competitor might be offering you.*

In this scenario, you need to know the value of your worth. In order to know and feel this, you should ideally already be in a job while negotiating an offer at another company. If you're looking for an internal promotion, you need to have offers from

---

* A worthwhile read on negotiation can be found in the book *Getting to Yes: Negotiating an Agreement Without Giving In* by Roger Fisher & William Ury.

elsewhere. If you are a free agent, you need to have multiple communications and offers from more than one employer.

Without multiple offers, an existing job or the confidence to set your own terms, you might reek of desperation because you need to take what you can get. You won't have the luxury of abundance that the other scenarios demonstrate or the ability or willingness to walk away. You have no other options. This is a weak bargaining position, and you are less likely to secure your desired outcome.

Be aware that the promotion you're after may well require you to leave your job. Recent studies showed that this is the most common way that workers gain better compensation than at their current place of work.*

I've been in a job for years – why haven't I been promoted?

If you want to be promoted or receive a pay rise, it's quite probable that you will need to engineer one. Many companies will automatically provide you with a single-digit percentage inflationary annual pay rise. This does not qualify as a promotion. In many instances, pay raises and promotions require a haggle.

* https://www.hrmagazine.co.uk/content/news/employees-quitting-jobs-due-to-lack-of-promotions/

Remember that companies want maximum profit margin, and employee salaries are a liability on their balance sheet. So, if you don't ask for a promotion, you probably won't get one. Don't be too scared to speak to your HR representative or manager about a promotion, or else you'll have to wait for someone else to leave or retire. And try to ask from a strong bargaining position, not a weak one!

I should also mention that sometimes there are factors beyond your control that mean you likely won't get a promotion with your current employer. Be it favouritism of certain colleagues over you, company politics or the economic climate at the time; sometimes a promotion simply isn't forthcoming. This might require you to look to a move elsewhere.

Can bonuses displace the need for a promotion?

Reliance on bonuses is risky business. They are usually tied to performance and are therefore discretionary. This means that in negotiation, you can be lured by the hope of great bonuses that may never materialise. Make sure you consider this when looking at jobs offering low base pay with good, but discretionary, bonuses. It's not something you can rely on and can leave you uncertain about your current and future financial position. Many lending banks will not factor in your bonus income for this reason. This can be important if you are looking to apply for a mortgage on a property, for example. Bonus payments are not certain and therefore the banks cannot assess your financials as reliable and assured when compared with the stability and regularity of a base salary.

Bonuses are also rarely paid promptly. Q1 bonuses can be paid in Q2 or Q3. Annual bonuses for the year prior are paid in early to mid-year. Sometimes bonus payments will be staggered – half now, half later.

Why do companies do this? It's because they want to enforce your loyalty to them by making you hang on for future bonus payments. If you have a future bonus coming, you are more likely to stay than leave. In most cases, if you resign before a bonus payment is made, the company will revoke the bonus, and you will have to forfeit it, even if it's for work you've already done and have therefore earned.

Delayed and staggered bonus payments are classic examples of the 'corporate handcuff.' The corporate handcuff is a term used for financial or other incentives that are distributed at some future date to incentivise employees' loyalty and longevity. Remember, companies spend resources educating and training personnel, and they do not want to lose them to the open market and competitors. They also want to retain employees at the lowest rates possible to maximise profit margins.

Other examples of the corporate handcuff include employee retention schemes of vesting equity distribution. In other words, the company promises the employee a reward for sticking around. For example, this could be a share package that's divided into quarters and paid over a period of four years. The employee unlocks 25 per cent of the vested shares at the end of each year worked until the fourth and final year of the package.

The corporate handcuff is not necessarily a bad thing, as many people will like the stability of the work and the associated delayed rewards. However, it is important to understand what the corporate handcuff is and why it is used. Make sure you consider that you might be tied to a job because of the corporate handcuff but that it offers no guarantees of promotion, increased responsibility or skill development during a vested time frame of several years. You need to consider whether this is in your best interest in the long term.

Are there any hidden dangers associated with promotion?

I used to work in a shop. Over the years, I have occasionally gone back as a customer and found that a store assistant I used to work with was still there and working the exact same job. They had declined promotion to store manager on several occasions. They were clearly happy to stay put, but I wonder whether they were really acting out of fear and self-doubt and taking the easy option. Perhaps there was more going on beneath the surface, but they were genuinely just happy to have the easiest, most stress-free version of 'work' there is.

I cannot, with a clean conscience, advise you to be happy with what you have and not try to grow and push yourself. It is not the mantra by which I go about my own career. However, be aware that with promotion comes more responsibility, including liability for the actions of others, and usually more pressure and expectation. I suspect that for most people, this is what they want, but some readers might prefer an easier life. More responsibility can mean longer working hours and less downtime to socialise with family and friends. With promotion comes heightened expectancy and new sets of rules and obligations associated with your work. It's not uncommon to feel as though you've bitten off more than you can chew at the start of your next chapter.

Am I really ready for a promotion?

Life happens fast, and it takes years for the mind to catch up with an ageing body. That's why the elderly are often heard saying they still feel young when their bodies suggest otherwise. We reach middle age quickly, yet we feel like we're still twenty-somethings. Some people respond to this dissonance with a mid-life crisis. They are reluctant to let go of their youth because they still feel and want to be a young adult despite their actual age saying otherwise. They have affairs with people half their age. They try to look and dress younger. They buy a sports car to feel 'cool.' They don't want to be old. Who does?

An alternative manifestation of this phenomenon is 'imposter syndrome.' One day, you might wake up and be in an important job, in a position of high responsibility, and freak out. Self-doubt creeps in, and you're not sure how you've made it this far. You undervalue your worth and find excuses for your prior successes, believing that you simply got 'lucky.' You doubt your ability to deliver on your responsibilities, some of which might be brand new.

You might feel generally insecure about your ability to perform at the level you find yourself at. You may be in a position of authority and responsibility, but don't feel as though you deserve to be there; you feel like an imposter. If you are suffering from imposter syndrome, you're probably in the majority of people who have risen through the ranks in their work.

The first thing to do is acknowledge that you are suffering from imposter syndrome, a well-known and very common insecurity in the careers of many. Label it exactly as it is.

Next, understand that there are several ways of dealing with it. One acquaintance once told me to 'fake it until I make it' when we discussed our experiences with imposter syndrome. Let's unpack this quote a little further.

If someone has promoted you or offered you a position of responsibility, it is because you have demonstrated something to them that merits it. It could be your experience, skills, personality or a combination of these. Anyone doing anything anywhere had a first time doing it. The world's greatest brain surgeon once sliced a scalpel into the lobe of a brain for the first time. An experienced airline pilot with tens of thousands of hours' experience took the yoke and once landed a plane for the first time. All hairdressers once took a pair of scissors and cut someone's hair for the first time. A tattoo artist once scratched some ink into someone's skin for the first time. Everyone who ever did anything good went from zero to hero. All of them. To be the hero, you need the zero.

Remember the growth zone? Well, look where we are here – well and truly outside of the comfort zone and in the depths of the growth zone. Whenever you feel imposter syndrome, treat it as an exciting opportunity for growth. In fact, it could even be time to celebrate when you feel discomfort because you know that rewards await you at the end of the road. You are about to gain growth, more experience and become an even better and more rounded version of yourself. How awesome is that? What an opportunity! Remember when you started your career at entry level or began a new job and felt like you knew nothing, and it was all quite overwhelming? This is the same thing. However, this time, you can look back and remember how you survived the challenge previously and subsequently prospered.

KEY TAKEAWAYS:

Most of us aspire for promotion in our jobs. This desire underpins a lot of what drives us to push forward and keep coming back each day. In this chapter, we've explored the qualities needed to be eligible for promotion and how to engineer promotion opportunities as well as bonuses, the corporate handcuff and how to deal with imposter syndrome. Below are some additional key takeaways:

- Promotions are awarded to those who demonstrate they have leadership qualities
- If you want a promotion, you'll most likely need to ask for one
- Grow and use your network. People remember the way you made them feel, and a strong network leads to promotion opportunities
- The strongest bargaining position is one where you are prepared to walk away
- Consider whether and how bonuses and the corporate handcuffs are influencing your mindset around promotion and career growth
- Imposter syndrome is an indication that you've entered the growth zone

Chapter 9

Navigating Career Crossroads and Career Changes

It's very likely that at some point in your career, you will need to pivot into something completely different. Such changes can be enforced by market conditions, such as your industry going through a downturn with multiple layoffs and hiring freezes, which forces you into a new direction. Other times, you may feel as though you've exhausted all the options that your industry has to offer, and your career trajectory has reached its finite conclusion. You might also have simply lost interest in your job and be looking for something new to escape boredom. Whatever the reason, moving into something new presents several challenges and can be very daunting, so in this chapter, we will dig a little deeper and examine why you may need to change your career and how to figure out what to do next.

How likely is it I will have to change careers?

Longevity in one job appears to be a thing of the past. In times gone by, many, if not most, people spent their entire careers at one company, spanning several decades until reaching retirement. In this day and age, although it still happens, it has become quite uncommon to find a single-company or single-job person. I put it down to a combination of increased global travel and relocation opportunities together with a shift in the macroeconomic environment as we move out of the industrial era and into the technological one. Here, changes happen far faster than in the past. Entire industries are being replaced or revolutionised. At one tech firm I worked for, the average tenure of employment was six months. I worked there for two years and was considered a veteran by the time I left.

A consequence of this evolution of workplace longevity is that most of us will need to navigate crossroads in our careers and consider the possibility of moving to other employers – if not different industries and professions altogether – multiple times during our working lives. It can seem scary, but I'd encourage you to see it as an exciting opportunity to broaden your life experience and embrace new challenges. Achieving a level of mastery in one field is awesome and should be respected, but why stop there? If you're absolutely passionate about your particular line of work and don't envisage your life going any other way, then you should always prioritise happiness and job satisfaction. However, if you want to sample different dishes from the buffet, the possibility of experiencing different types of work provides the opportunity to broaden your life story and become more well-rounded. It's also possible to try out different careers at one company – this is something I have seen before, too. People join one department and several years later are working at the same employer but with an entirely different scope of work. This is also something to consider.

<u>Is it a bad thing to have had too many jobs?</u>

When browsing CVs as a hiring manager, one thing that stands out like a sore thumb is the brevity of time spent in jobs by some individuals. Evidence of 'job hopping' leaves a subconscious concern that a candidate has not found something they like doing or that they lack loyalty. It begs the question of whether they are worth training because there may be no return on that investment. There is an unspoken expectation that a person should be in a job for at least one to two years at a time, if not longer. A former colleague from Switzerland once told me that the minimum expected term there is three years. Be mindful of this number relative to your location and consider how you would discuss it with a hiring manager who questions the duration of your prior working engagements. The same sentiment applies to large gaps between jobs. You can expect to be questioned over these and should have a valid answer, such as taking time out to study, maternity or paternity leave and so on.

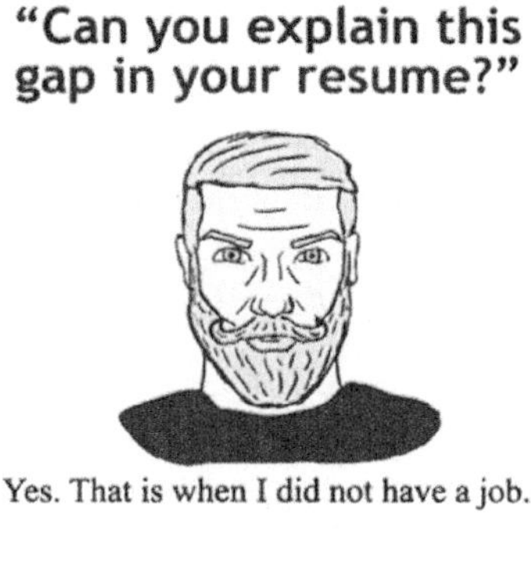

There are some exceptions to the need to remain in roles for a couple of years at a time. The technology start-up scene is rife with developers who work short stints on different projects; brief employment relationships are normal in this industry. Additionally, some types of work are inherently short-lived, such as fixed-term contracts, maternity cover, consultancy, contracting and agency work. These roles are all defensible against the perceived sin of job-hopping.

What should I do when I feel like my job has run its course?

You may reach a point in your career where you feel there is nothing else for you to accomplish in your company or line of work. This could be due to the structure of the company hierarchy and career progression (for example, you won't get promoted unless someone higher up leaves or retires) or because you feel like you've learnt and experienced as much as you can in your particular field. Some people are happy to maintain this position as the years roll by. If you're like me, you need to feel as though you're always moving forward. You need to be continually learning new things and progressing.

Once you've learnt all you can, you're in a predicament. Maintain the status quo, and you will find yourself in the stagnation zone. Here, you're at risk of diminished job satisfaction because you're no longer being challenged or achieving new milestones. Part of what makes work rewarding is the feeling that you're building towards some achievement and can observe the progress you make. If you cannot visualise a viable future, it's time to reconsider your position.

At this point, you have several options. You can stay with your present employer and seek an internal transfer to another team or field within the wider organisation. This will provide you with new opportunities and challenges without needing to partake in the rigmarole of job hunting. You will additionally remain in familiar surroundings. If this option is not possible or desirable, you need to consider moving to another employer.

Why do I feel hesitant about career change?

You're considering leaving something familiar and reliable for the abyss of the unknown. You are moving away from your comfort zone! When I was younger, I used to think that a career change meant starting from scratch. I saw it as a complete disposal of everything accomplished up to that point. And while there is indeed an element of starting again, you absolutely do not lose the life experience, interpersonal skills, wisdom and network that you've thus far established.

Career change is difficult and incites a degree of fear, but you're not restarting as a complete newbie to the workforce. Instead, you're entering the scene as a seasoned pro with a hell of a lot to offer. This will bode extremely well for you because you'll be able to win the trust of key stakeholders and get up to speed much quicker in your new field than someone with no track record.

Think of the person you were ten years ago. You've changed a lot since then. You will have developed new interests, new priorities and new pursuits. Take stock of the idea that who you are today is not who you will be in ten years, either.

What should I do next?

I cannot advise you what to move into. That is entirely dependent on you as a unique individual. When I transitioned into a career in the financial markets, my interest was sparked by my love of sports. Sports and sporting outcomes tend to revolve around different patterns. I've watched thousands of hours of sports in my life and observed the various patterns at play in sporting contests. The way patterns form and repeat over time is strangely repetitive and predictable. This sparked an unshakeable curiosity in me. When I noticed that financial markets also work in a similar way, I had to find out more.

'The only way to be truly satisfied is to do what you believe is great work. And the only way to do great work is to love what you do. If you haven't found it yet, keep looking. Don't settle. As with all matters of the heart, you'll know when you find it.'

Steve Jobs

Am I too old to start anew?

'That's not me' and 'I'm too old to start a new career' are excuses people give when they are afraid of change and trying something new. You are *choosing* to frame the situation that way. It might not be you now, but it could be you in future if you are prepared to apply yourself accordingly. I always said that working in sales was not for me because I disliked the idea of rejection that salespeople endure on a daily basis. However, not only did I end up working in a sales position for several years, but I thrived in it and enjoyed the challenge. Never underestimate the value of placing yourself in the growth zone.

'YOLO – You Only Live Once.'

Unknown

Many religions preach about the concept of the afterlife, which materialises in various forms. Heaven, hell, purgatory and reincarnation. Whatever your spiritual inclination, most people believe in only one physical life on earth. You probably only have one shot at this. If humans only ever have one life, then it's vital to take advantage of this precious opportunity to experience and achieve the endless options out there. The same goes for work. One day, you will retire and look back on your life, including your working life, and will be in a position to reflect. The pain of regret is profound, so try to minimise any regrets around your career by exploring all the things you want to encounter in life.

Another misconception I've heard is that 'this is a young person's game.' People with this perception presume that employers don't want to hire people in the middle or tail-end of their careers because it inhibits a return on investment that would be better suited to a younger person with more working runway ahead of them. When interviewing for an internship in my thirties, I was asked why I applied for the role given that all the other applications they received were from recent graduates a decade or more younger than me. I replied that I hadn't found something I was passionate about, until now. By being truthful and exposing what was behind my hunger to pursue this opportunity I was offered the job.

An older, wiser and experienced head has many advantages over a younger one. Life experience, maturity, and experience in different jobs, industries and work cultures, to name a few examples. The ability to coach and train younger colleagues is additionally something that younger colleagues cannot offer! These factors can enable you to nullify the arguments against hiring older people. Older folks have a bigger network to take advantage of and can offer various ways of contributing to a company.

Every single person has something to offer and some value to add. You are never too old to try something new. Don't talk yourself out of trying things because you perceive yourself to be too old. There's a reason why companies hire non-executive directors. These people tend to be in the latter stages of their careers and have a repertoire of valuable experience across many areas. Their advice and suggestions at the board level are priceless to companies navigating dilemmas, predicaments and strategies. Not everyone can or wants to become a non-executive director, but the point remains that age can be a benefit rather than a hindrance. Depending on what you decide to do, remember that if you want to restart in a new career, you might need to accept a lower salary than you're used to.

'As with all matters of the heart, you'll know when you find it.'

How will *I* know?

You'll know when you've found your next steps when you feel like you're compelled to take them. Where motivation is a feeling of *wanting* to do something, compulsion is the feeling of *having* to do it. There are, of course, examples in which compulsion stems from financial responsibility towards others, such as having a family to support, needing somewhere to live, having bills to pay and so on. Setting aside the requirement to have an income, compulsion in this context is an exciting need to pursue the work.

The best and most fun jobs are those ones where your motivation, desire and excitement compel you to pursue them. It feels right in your soul. You feel that you were born to do it. When making career decisions, you must discover what compels you and run with that feeling whenever possible. That combination of hunger and excitement creates a very rewarding aura around your work and leads to the highest sense of career fulfilment.

You might love sewing jumpers and scarves and decide that the textiles industry is where your curiosity lies. You might love science and decide that you need to explore the world of science-fiction storytelling. What I'm suggesting is that you think about what really interests you and find a line of work with some link to it. The work itself might be entirely different to the underlying passion or hobby, but that link is where you discover what drives and motivates you deep down and what will help you get into a line of work that you're really going to enjoy and thrive at doing. Enjoying your work is even more critical when your motivation wanes, and you need to find another reason to keep pushing forward towards your career goals.

What if I don't want to change?

'It is not the strongest of the species that survives, not the most intelligent that survives. It is the one that is the most adaptable to change.'

Charles Darwin

Charles Darwin rose to fame through his theory of evolution. In extremely simplified terms, the theory of evolution is one of survival of the fittest. Those with the strongest genes and physical characteristics survived in their environment over those with weaker qualities and, therefore, reproduced their genes and characteristics through their offspring. The strong survived, and the weak died and became extinct, along with their genetic code.

Fast-forward through millions of years, and today, we see a world of different species that all survived because they possess the traits required to do so. However, the critical piece of this puzzle is that being the strongest in any given moment means nothing if one is incapable of adapting to dynamically changing surroundings.

The world in which we now live is always changing. We have already discussed the speed at which this is now happening due to the technological era we have entered into. As technology is capable of processing information much faster than the human brain, combined with the fact that computers can learn from the information that they are fed, the law of accelerated returns (Kurzweil's law) will apply.

The law of accelerated returns can be simplified as particular methods working better than others. The methods that work are filtered out from the others that do not and are then used to develop the next stage of progress. With the processing power of technology, positive feedback can be received and interpreted faster than ever before, meaning the next stage of progress can be achieved quickly. As more and more positive feedback is extracted from the world, efficiency is going to become more enhanced and exponential growth will happen faster and more profoundly.

This is a deep rabbit hole, and my intention is not to evoke feelings of anxiety and fear but rather to make you aware of what is happening if you don't already know. It can be a worrying subject matter for some, but I cannot write material on career mindset without highlighting the reality of what's to come. I hope this will stimulate some forward-thinking consideration of how to hone your career path selection process. It would be prudent to consider which jobs are facing future extinction.

The hope is that technology will make the world a more efficient and better place, but it will surely also make many careers and perhaps entire industries redundant. In the absence of universal basic income, a social welfare mechanism where all citizens receive unconditional income from the state without the need to work, it will be necessary to adapt to this reality and use it to inform your career choice.

How can I transition into something different?

Moving into something new will require varying degrees of education. You are, after all, going to need to develop new skills or qualities. This education might come in the form of studying an accredited course. In other instances, you'll be trained while at work by your new employer or organisation. It will depend entirely on your circumstances, but an education of some kind will almost certainly be required. Of course, if you've found your calling, it will be much easier to complete this process because you'll be learning about something you *want* to learn about.

How this happens will depend on where you are in your life. If you are still at home living with your parents, your financial obligations may be lower, and you'll find it easier to make this transition. If you have financial responsibilities such as children, a mortgage, rent or other living expenses, then you'll need to adapt your schedule to cover both bases. That means your evenings and weekends (spare time) will take on a whole new meaning.

If you've been able to save up some spare cash, you may have enough in the bank to cover your financial obligations and possible tuition costs to take a timeout from work to develop new skills. Perhaps you have a partner who can carry the financial burden for a time. Alternatively, you'll need to develop skills in your spare time while maintaining your existing income streams. Nobody said it was going to be easy, but most things worth doing in life rarely are. If you've found something that really stirs your interest, then it'll be a worthwhile means to an end.

I'm going to recall a story from my time spent in Australia. I needed work badly, and I befriended someone who helped me into a new job. They worked for a catering company which needed a driver to make food deliveries, so I agreed to work for them. Upon turning up on my first day, they showed me to my vehicle. It was a pretty large truck. I'd never driven anything larger than a camper van before. I showed them my driving licence because I wasn't sure it covered a vehicle of this size, but they insisted it did. So, I accepted the job and started driving a truck around Melbourne that I didn't feel at all comfortable driving.

The person who helped me into the job was a chef for the same company. Only they weren't really a chef. They took the role of chef without any prior experience and would Google the recipes for meals they needed to cook while working. This story is pretty funny to me, looking back. You had a truck driver who didn't know how to drive trucks and a chef who didn't know how to cook. The moral of this story is not to tell you to deceive anybody for work – do not break the law! The moral here is to use some initiative when you're stuck in a predicament and need to resort to creative ways to instigate something new.

What if I'm faced with layoffs and redundancies?

Lots of industries go through cycles of good periods and bad. Businesses experience times of growth and consolidation. Some professions offer more stability than others, but there are no guarantees. Doctors could be replaced by robots; airline pilots could be grounded by pandemics; lawyers could be made redundant by cryptocurrency smart contracts. Market forces can be disruptive to career stability, and even the biggest and most profitable businesses can enter bankruptcy if the tide turns. Layoffs and redundancies are common, and many people have to navigate through them.

Moments like these, when businesses struggle, are why you build your 'rainy day' fund. Hopefully you have some short- to mid-term financial security to cover your costs while you take some time to digest and review your position and decide what to do next. You may decide you never want to be in this position again and start your own business where you're not at the mercy of a hiring (or firing) manager. Alternatively, if you loved your job, you might see this as a bump in the road that is *necessary* on your journey to success and find another similar job. Success depends on failure, and bumps in the road are a necessity (more on that in the next chapter). How exciting for you that this moment is a reminder that you are on that path to glory!

If you are facing redundancy, make sure to research any financial relief available to you from the state or whether there are any guaranteed minimum notice periods and processes that are required by your employer. Your employer should advise you and keep you informed, but it is worth doing some research into what your basic rights are.

Being laid off feels like failure - how can I view it differently?

'Luck is what happens when preparation meets opportunity.'

Seneca, Roman Philosopher

I am a firm believer in the above quote. You could also adapt the phrase to state that success happens when preparation meets opportunity. Until now, you've developed and grown as a person. What feels like a failure should be construed as an opportunity. You cannot control every detail of your life, let alone your career, and sometimes you can be dealt a bad card. Not only have you (hopefully) prepared for such instances financially, but you have grown your network, skills and experience to be able to seize any opportunities that come your way. Opportunities usually come your way because you have put yourself in a position to receive them and are ready to pounce when the moment arrives. Putting yourself in that position requires hustle.

Hustle

To hustle is to pursue something both rapidly and energetically. Pick up your phone and call those in your network who could help you. Reach out to people you have never met before. Send a direct message to someone on LinkedIn who has your ideal job and ask them for a chat. Do this with ten different people, and one might agree to pick up the phone and offer their wisdom. Ask for an introduction to new people who are connected to those in your network. Find and use your community. If you sit and wait for the phone to ring, it probably never will. Luck and success happen when preparation meets opportunity. Opportunities often need to be carved out.

Preparation

'By failing to prepare, you are preparing to fail.'
Benjamin Franklin

The concept of preparation should extend beyond simply doing your homework. Of course, having sound knowledge of a particular subject will be important. But the wider context here is to put to use the skills, experience, maturity and network you have established up to this point so that when an opportunity presents itself you're ready to seize it. Preparation includes being able to demonstrate all of your qualities, not just the subject matter itself. If you are looking at starting a new business, it could mean that you have identified a gap in a particular market or are able to solve a critical problem you discovered when at work and now is the time to execute your solution. With sufficient preparation, you will be able to convincingly propose your solution to a problem to the right people.

Stay positive

We spoke earlier about the power of positive thinking and the law of attraction. If you've been able to harness these superpowers in the past, then you'll know how they can help to put you in a position of strength. Continue doing this. If you've never practised positive thinking, there's no better time to start than when navigating a career crossroads. You have absolutely nothing to lose by trying it, and you might be surprised by how a positive mentality helps you receive great opportunities. If you keep doing what you've always done, you'll keep getting what you've always gotten, whatever that means for you.

KEY TAKEAWAYS:

In this chapter we looked at career crossroads and career change. It's certainly a sticky situation, but one that many of us will have to navigate through at some point. We looked at why career crossroads come about, how to react to them and what to do next. Additionally, remember that:

- Career change is very common and presents a defining opportunity
- You may have to pivot multiple times in your career
- Career change can happen due to natural expiration in a job or industry or because of market forces and layoffs
- When determining what to do next, you should consider what you enjoy and seek work with some connection to this
- You'll know when you've made the right choice (and when you have not)
- If necessary, use your initiative to kick-start your next career move
- The world is changing faster than ever before – and this requires you to keep changing, too
- You must treat failure as an opportunity
- Your next move will come about through hustle, preparation and a positive mindset

Chapter 10

Discovering the Truth About Success

Success can be simplified as achieving an outcome you pursued. This can be an objective as small as completing a puzzle or something as large as winning an Olympic gold medal. The reward and satisfaction of success is what drives us to it in the first place. Achieving success can be wonderful, but there's a lot more to it than that. In this chapter, we will look at what success really means, how to achieve it and where your focus should be when pursuing it.

Should I judge my success against other people?

Comparing yourself with other people is dangerous. For all the inspiration that can be gained from others, it can also be highly demoralising and demotivating to compare your life and successes with theirs. Seeing the riches of someone you perceive to be successful can get you down, make you feel inadequate and introduce self-doubt. Remember that your view of people and their success is a result of your own perception of them. In reality, their life may be completely different to what you are presuming.

Some of my friends like to bet on sport, and they are quick to share news of their fortunes when they win. But I know that for every win, there are countless losses. Losses which probably exceed their wins by some margin. I never see the losses because they never share them. On the face of it, it would seem that they have a knack for calling the right outcome on a frequent basis. How on earth do they do it? They don't. Beneath the surface are multiple instances in which they get it terribly wrong. Even when people appear victorious, there's a chance that they're anything but. There is a danger of interpreting others' successes the wrong way and feeling inadequate for it. Many additionally end up setting unrealistic expectations of themselves.

It's absolutely vital to focus on your path, process and journey and to not pay too much attention to others. Feel free to cherry-pick inspiration from them, but it need not go much deeper than that. You should seek whatever success means to you, not what someone else has accomplished. Compare yourself with yourself and where you were three months ago, a year ago, five years ago. This is where you'll discover the progress you've made and the affirmation that your process is working.

What is the journey to success really like?

I have this image printed on a canvas on my desk. It acts as a reminder that there will be several bumps in the road, setbacks, suffering, blood, sweat and tears before accomplishing something important. Getting to that finish line will not be easy.

When viewing the successes of others, it can seem so easy. It's also easy to presume that they must be a natural or have had a bit of good luck go their way. They went after something, and they got it. If only it were that simple.

For every success story an entrepreneur has, there are several failures to accompany it. New products experience teething issues before they are perfected. Innovation stumbles multiple times before it succeeds for the betterment of mankind. We see images of Olympic gold medallists standing proud on a podium, but we do not see the preceding four years of training they endured and all the associated pain, injuries and sacrifices that go with it.

Space rockets are launched and crash back down to earth many times before finally achieving stable orbit. I recently watched SpaceX's inaugural rocket launch of its Starship prototype. The Starship is what Elon Musk intends to use as the vehicle that will take humans to Mars in the future. The launch itself was successful, but minutes later, upon reaching the outer atmosphere, the ship's rocket system failed to separate as planned, and the structure exploded spectacularly. What struck me about this was that despite the explosion, there was an eruption of cheers and congratulations in the control centre. The launch was declared a success by SpaceX. Yet I had friends who didn't understand messaging me about how it could possibly be a success, given that it exploded less than four minutes into its flight.

The team in the control centre knew that simply launching the Starship itself was of enormous importance to the overall process of achieving a stable orbit in future. There were huge lessons learnt, and feedback gained about what they need to do next time to go one step further. Musk himself congratulated his team, having previously declared only a 50 per cent expectation that the Starship would achieve orbit.

Credit: X (Formerly Twitter): @elonmusk

He adjusted his expectation of achieving orbit later in 2023 to 80 per cent.

Once you truly accept that setbacks *will* happen, something magical happens. You begin to understand that not only will they happen, but they *must* happen for you to be successful. Success *depends* on multiple failures and bumps in the road. It's how we learn, process feedback and identify the weaknesses we need to work on. This magic manifests as a realisation that the very experience of failures and setbacks themselves is a moment to be celebrated. Sure, something bad has happened, and you are allowed to hurt. That's part of the game and part of human emotion. But rather than allowing it to be a terminal setback, you can frame it entirely differently. If you *know* that setbacks and failures are *required* to become successful later, then encountering those setbacks is an indicator that you're experiencing what all successful people go through on the road to success.

I was playing a game with my daughter recently that I hadn't played in years: snakes and ladders. In case you haven't encountered it before, it's a board game where players roll a dice and the number it lands on determines how many spaces forward you can move. The first to reach one hundred on the board wins. Some numbers on the board are the bottom rung of a ladder. Landing on these means you can bypass a number of squares to land on a square much closer to one hundred. The problem is that other spaces have the head of a snake. If you land on those, you need to slide back down to the tail of the snake and the associated square and go again. I'm not sure if the inventors of this game were considering the path to success, but it is quite a fitting example of it

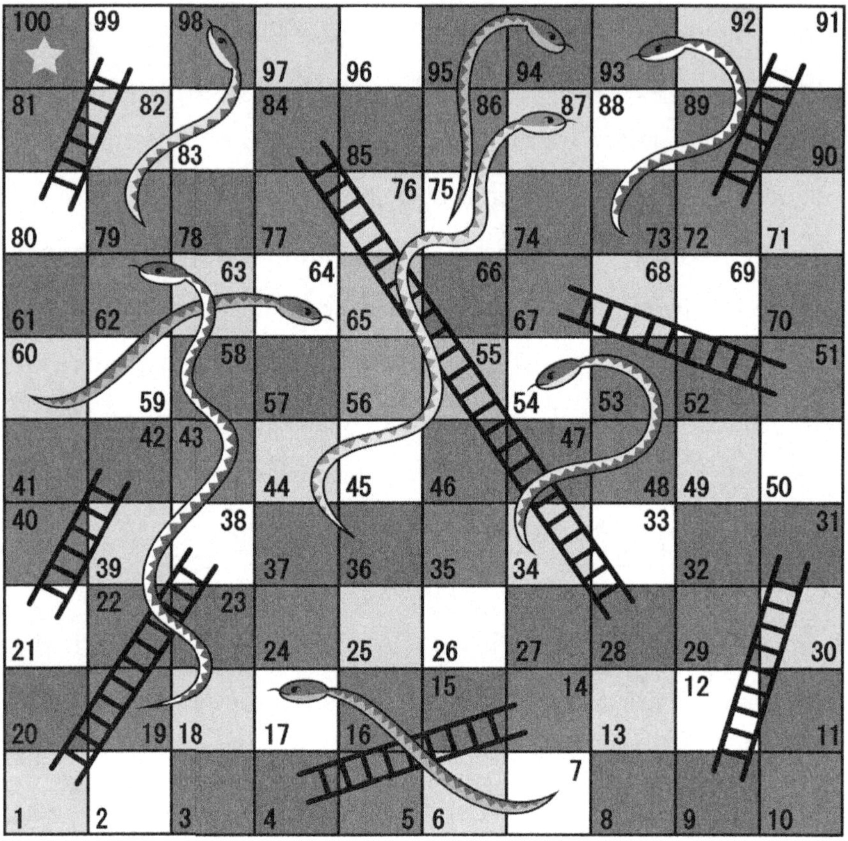

Remember the importance of learning from other people's mistakes. In the game of snakes and ladders, the snakes represent the setbacks we all face, while the ladders represent the lessons we can learn from the mistakes and failures of others. In doing

so, we can expedite our learning curve and bypass those mistakes altogether.

What does success really mean?

There's a common misconception that once you achieve something, you'll be satisfied. There's a finality to this belief. Closure. You've done it! But truly successful people never lose their hunger to achieve. You may pick up multiple wins along the way, but there's always another challenge around the corner. The satisfaction you feel from your successes will fuel your desire to have more. After a while, the rush from the win will fade away. Then what? Once you've made your first million, are you really happy there? Or do you want more? If you can establish a net worth of a million, why not try and make it ten? Maybe wealth is not all it's cracked up to be, and you alter the way you frame success into helping the world instead. That's a new challenge altogether, and success in that setting will look entirely different. Success is not final – there's always room for more.

What is the fastest way to be successful?

Time is your friend, not your enemy. Being good at something usually does not come naturally to people. It requires patience, practice and consistency. Doing it over and over again until you do it well. This process requires time. It takes years to be considered an expert in any line of work. This is because you need to experience enough things to fully understand what it means to ply your trade to a high standard. Time is your friend because it enables the experiences you need to become good at something to happen. Do you really want to be a movie director before you've ever stepped foot on a film set? Knowing that things take time to master allows you to enjoy the process and will afford you the opportunity to become good at what you're seeking to master.

What does success feel like?

Success is often beautiful and euphoric. You might have set out to accomplish something difficult that not many are able to. The satisfaction gets your feel-good hormones flowing, and you revel in the glow of victory. The reward is one of fulfilment. Sometimes success can feel like relief because of the difficulties you endured to make it there. You're glad you've 'won,' but it doesn't feel as good as you hoped it might. Perhaps something you thought would take months actually took years to accomplish, or for whatever reason, the finish line doesn't quite hit your dopamine receptors like other victories did and do. This can feel underwhelming and even anti-climactic.

This feedback is worth analysing and should not be ignored. You might put it down to process fatigue or becoming jaded. Or perhaps what you did, while initially being something you thought you wanted to do, is something you've realised you're not so concerned about having accomplished now that you have done so. Perhaps there was an absence of fun along the way, or the rewards weren't worth the effort. If you're feeling this way about a moment of success, make sure you listen to your internal feedback mechanism. It may be that what you think you need to be happy is really something else altogether.

Upon appearing in the Wimbledon men's tennis final in 2022, Australian player Nick Kyrgios was asked if it made him hungry for more finals. His reply was very interesting:

'Absolutely not. I'm so tired, honestly. Myself, my team, I think we're all exhausted. We have played so much tennis.'

Does being rich make me successful?

If you define success as being rich, then you are successful by your own definition. The problem is that people often make the mistake of thinking that money will lead to happiness when the truth is that money will lead to freedom. I've observed that many wealthy people are also deeply unhappy individuals. When we read about these people, their net worth is often quoted somewhere in the dialogue; however, have you not also read about the many successful people who have needed to check into rehab? In fact, many, if not most, stories about successful people are talking not of their successes but of their unhappiness and problems. Addiction, divorce, bankruptcy and the downsides of fame are not stories of happiness. It's no good being rich and miserable.

When I was younger, I believed that you could not be successful without being rich. If I could be rich one day, then I could be happy. As I've grown older, I'm under no illusion that any money I make will make me happy. In fact, some of the most enjoyable periods of my career have been while not earning great money. What I absolutely loved in those moments was my dedication to the journey. Sometimes I was making good money but had low job satisfaction. Other times, I have been compensated well for my achievements, but that was always a nice by-product of what was otherwise a rewarding process.

You can have a bunch of things on your bucket list, and the easiest way for you to be able to go after those things is by having the financial freedom that will enable you to do so. Money does not guarantee happiness; it unlocks the freedom to pursue bold and adventurous goals while minimising the financial risk associated with failure.

What is happiness?

Understanding the meaning of happiness is essential to knowing what version of 'success' to pursue. Is success possible in the absence of happiness? Objectively, you could argue it is. A gold-medal Olympian is undoubtedly successful. The real question is whether going after success is worth it if you can't be happy at the same time. Staying in a glamorous and well-paying job that's destroying your health and joy in life is not conducive to happiness. That's why it's crucial to pursue success and happiness together while understanding that one does not guarantee the other. Happiness comes from within, and shiny new objects or status-enhancing accomplishments usually provide temporary happiness or even relief from your true reality.

Real happiness arrives from being at peace with yourself and who you really are. Only you can know whether you're in that state and if you're at peace with yourself. The only thing you can control in life is yourself, nothing else. Therefore, it's important to work on whatever baggage you're carrying in order to liberate yourself from whatever is impeding your happiness. For example, I know a lot of folks who are unhappy because they are living a life they were pressured into living by others. This means they're not being true to themselves, and this conflict causes a constant internal battle.

Accepting uncertainty and your inability to change lots of things about the world and other people are fundamental aspects of happiness. Dissatisfaction with these things will hinder your happiness because of a desire to change them but an inability to ever do so. I've been fortunate enough to have made many friends from all over the world. I've travelled to different continents to spend time with them in their environments. These were valuable life experiences that might not have happened without my acceptance that these people are all very different to me. It's possible to find fault in every single person walking the earth. They are flawed, like you and I, and by begrudging them for their flaws, you're blocking out the opportunity to connect with them because they're imperfect, just like you. By accepting the things you cannot change, you remove this burden upon yourself, freeing up and enabling the possibility of happiness and positivity. This mantra flows into your career prospects because of how important your network and connections will be over time. Aim for success *and* happiness.

Sometimes the pursuit of success and happiness will require you to endure some pain. Pain is something we all seek to avoid. Pain hurts, after all, so it makes sense that we try to avoid it! However, this is too much of a generalisation. Certain forms of physical and mental pain are most definitely bad for us. Other types of pain are forms of temporary suffering that will lead to growth. It's important to realise this distinction and analyse which pain should be avoided and which is temporary. The former type of pain is harmful, but the latter is often highly beneficial.

What is the most important thing I should be focusing on?

'Concentrate on what will produce results rather than on the results, the process rather than the prize.'

Bill Walsh

We have seen how the journey to success is littered with pain, difficulty, obstacles and setbacks. Good times and bad. If you only allow yourself to enjoy the finish line, you're inviting misery onto your journey at worst and apathy at best. You will end up denying happiness until you reach the final prize. This seems especially daft if the feeling you get at the end of completing certain goals is underwhelming. Attaining an achievement is simply a single moment in the larger process. There is so much time exhausted between the start and the end. Always living in the future (or indeed the past) means you are disregarding the present. Seek out the beauty of the process itself to enjoy the journey.

Once you embrace the fact that your endurance and consistency are what will enable you to achieve your goals, you can enjoy each moment and celebrate the small victories along the way. This will feed your perseverance and persistence.

<u>What do you wish you could tell your younger self?</u>

This question is posted on online forums I follow from time to time, and I'm always fascinated by the responses. Here are some valuable answers I've read:

- Enjoy this moment because you'll never get it back
- Be kinder to yourself
- Don't allow your fears to hold you back
- Don't be in a rush to have life figured out
- Enjoy the process, or else life will pass you by
- You have unique gifts. Use them
- You didn't travel enough
- You spend too much time worrying
- You didn't take enough career chances or risks
- Be a better spouse, parent or friend
- Do more for others

Imagine having a conversation with a child or young adult who is asking you for life lessons. What would you tell them? Is it too late to listen to your own advice? Learning from others and then passing on those teachings is a core part of the cycle of life.

KEY TAKEAWAYS:

In this chapter we explored the truth about success. We unravelled how it can manifest differently, where to focus your priorities and how to achieve the ultimate success – happiness. Below are the key takeaways:

- Stop comparing yourself with other people. You don't know what goes on in their lives behind closed doors. Figure out what success means for *you* and chase it
- The journey to success is littered with ups and downs, and failure is a critical part of it – *that* is the game
- When trying to figure out what success means to you, don't be surprised to find out that some iterations of it aren't what you'd hoped they'd be
- Money unlocks freedom, not happiness
- Success and happiness are independent of one another
- Your sense of happiness can only come from within yourself – you can only feel truly content if you are at peace with yourself
- If you only focus on a final outcome, you are missing out on the journey
- Ask yourself if you are honouring your lessons to your younger self

Chapter 11

Being Inspired and Inspiring Others

Learning from others helps us navigate through predicaments without needing to fail at something ourselves. Note here that there is a distinction between comparing your fortunes with others and learning from their wisdom.

We all look up to leaders in our lives, be it a parent, politician or others in our community. Sometimes, you'll observe an accomplishment of theirs, and it will *really* stir up your interest in it to the point of wanting to go after that thing yourself. This brings me to the concept of inspiration.

Inspiration in this context not only looks at *what* amazing thing somebody did but also, and perhaps more importantly, *how* they did it. It's the combination of their accomplishing something great while also understanding the sacrifices and hurdles they had to overcome to get it. The awe we feel when inspired by others comes from subconsciously understanding that they went through a process and journey to make it happen. We're shown the end-product of what they've done, but their outcome is usually a by-product of their processes and methods. By finding out how they did it, we can begin to understand what is required of us to achieve the same feats.

In this chapter, we will examine the various sources of inspiration available to us, the value we should ascribe to the teachings of different people and the understanding that we need to play our role to inspire those who will follow in our footsteps.

Where should I look for inspiration?

Talk to successful people. Find people in your family, your extended circle of friends, senior executives at work or anyone else you have access to who has 'made it' – whatever 'made it' means to you. Pick their brains and ask them how they did it. What was their process, their journey? How did they fail? How did they learn from and respond to their failures? What risks did they take?

I want advice from these people over anybody else. Some of them won't give you the time of day, but you'll be surprised by how many will be happy to set aside some time for you. If you have access to such people, it's a resource you should make the most of.

How important are leaders as sources of inspiration?

One role of a leader is to guide. To take your hand and show you not only what to do but how to go about doing it. Until we achieve mastery in something, we can use and look up to leaders to demonstrate what mastery truly looks like.

A bad leader often abuses their position of authority for their own personal gain. They disregard the requirement to guide others and focus solely on themselves. We see bad leaders in politics especially, and regardless of whatever part of the world you're in, you'll be able to think of several examples in your local community. However, the workplace can be a hotbed of bad leaders, too.

Good leaders make you want to become better at your job and also in your life in general. How do they do this? Not only are they good at what they do, but they set targets and go after them while leading by example and helping others with similar aspirations. Good leaders build trust by demonstrating selflessness and by defending others in their cohort. They understand that they have dependents who look up to them, and they revel in the responsibility of making those around them better. Instead of focusing solely on themselves, they understand that uplifting others is a widely respected trait that transcends their individual achievements alone. They get you to buy into their vision and ambitions by encouraging you and setting the tone themselves. Do you think business owners prefer leaders who can perform at the expense of others or those whose performance is supplemented by an associated group of high performers? We want to take inspiration from good leaders, not bad ones.

Are all leaders the same?

Leaders are capable of positively influencing your learning curve in different ways. Let's compare the 'peacetime CEO' and the 'wartime CEO,' a concept created by Ben Horowitz, a Silicon Valley venture capitalist. Both roles entail different leadership qualities during variable and dynamic business climates.

Peacetime refers to a climate where business is booming, and a company has a large advantage against its competition. You might find your business is in the right place at the right time and is in a position to capitalise on a growing market seeking the exact products or services you offer. Jackpot! Leaders in this position should be looking to capitalise as much as possible to maximise revenue and growth.

Wartime refers to a climate in which the business is under imminent existential threat and the survival of the company is in doubt. Leaders in this position should be looking for ways to bring the company out of a doomsday predicament. The solution takes the form of a creative, lateral or even disruptive strategy. In other words, evolve or die. Charles Darwin taught that those species that adapt best to their changing environment have the best chance of surviving.

While both types of leaders have important qualities, I have heard many people attribute the most value to the wartime CEO. I have experienced both business climates, and what I have taken from them is it is really hard to go wrong during peacetime so long as you sail with the wind. Revenue is strong and steady, and it would really require gross negligence or incompetence for things to go horribly wrong. The peacetime CEO looks successful because their business is flying. Shareholders are happy because company targets are met or exceeded, and the balance sheet looks great.

The wartime CEO is a person who steps up in the face of adversity when the going gets tough. Those who are able to navigate their businesses out of existential threat are priceless because they can lead their team to a successful outcome while sailing *into* the wind. They manage to find a solution when the stakes are highest. One of the reasons that Steve Jobs is so widely revered is that he managed to steer Apple to prosperity after being mere weeks away from bankruptcy.

This is not a dig at peacetime CEOs, by the way. There is a huge importance that should be attributed to the opportunities presented by peacetime. Maximisation of revenue in these times could be the difference between survival of future existential threats or failure, as market cycles mean there may be leaner times ahead in the company's future and that it only survives due to its ability to make the most of the preceding good times. It is important to use and learn from the strengths of each and every good leader we encounter while understanding that they will all have different qualities.

How can people stay inspired after experiencing failure?

Looking at how successful people respond to failure is where you will *really* be able to source inspiration. As the opposite of success, failure is a consequence of setting out to do something but ultimately not accomplishing it. I have already set out why failures are inevitable, valuable and needed. But their value is only realised when interpreted correctly.

'Fool me once, shame on you. Fool me twice, shame on me. Fool me three times, shame on both of us.'

Stephen King

It is OK to fail, but not assessing or acting on why you failed is not. This is a recipe for failing repeatedly. You cannot expect a different outcome if you do not use the feedback failure made available to you.

'Failure isn't fatal, but failure to change might be.'

John Wooden

Part of what makes people inspirational is their response to failure. They figure out where they went wrong and take ownership of the outcomes. They look for explanations, not excuses. Excuses apportion the responsibility of failure to external factors beyond your control. External causes may have been contributory factors, but what could you do better to mitigate against them in future? When failing at something, seek to understand why the failure happened and what you can do to improve. Perpetual failure will happen until you conduct this analysis and make a change.

'Failure should be our teacher, not our undertaker. Failure is delay, not defeat. It is a temporary detour, not a dead end. Failure is something we can avoid only by saying nothing, doing nothing, and being nothing.'
Denis Waitley

Embrace your failures and accept responsibility for them. Learn from them and make the changes needed to avoid making the same mistakes in future. This is how you can use failures to fuel your progress and success.

How helpful are social media influencers for inspiration?

It's important here to highlight the distinction between inspirational leaders and influencers. While it is possible for a person to be both at the same time, influencers are very often looking to grow their community for some commercial return. Whether that be by selling their own products or services or advertising on behalf of others to their audience.

Social media influencers are those who have established credibility and reputation about a certain subject or set of subjects, culminating in their amassing a 'following' on social media. As more people follow them, they build entire communities of hundreds, thousands or millions of people. They then become attractive to issuers of products and services looking to market to large groups of people.

Social media influencers often pose generic questions to elicit responses from their community without any advisory input themselves. There is even now a defined area of the marketing industry called 'influencer marketing.' Here, the influencer is trying to persuade you to make a financial commitment to something that they take a commission from. Just bear that in mind when considering the value of their influence on you. Does their influence serve you in the right way? Are they helping you? Remember the importance of not comparing yourself to other people when quantifying your own success. It's important to be inspired by the right people. While someone may have amassed a huge following on social media, do they really provide a positive influence on you in ways that will help you grow as a person?

How can older generations inspire younger ones?

Children are the leaders of tomorrow. Therefore, older generations are bestowed with the duty to encourage and inspire their development positively and productively.

Today, things are changing very rapidly over shorter periods of time than ever before, and with that comes a gulf in interest and participation between younger and older generations in regard to new technological advancements. I've observed that older folks tend to be less savvy with new technology. However, this is down to the fact that education in and awareness of technology simply didn't exist during their foundational years in the same way it does today. Children and young adults possess a more rigorous curiosity in new things, and trends tend to spread more rapidly throughout younger generations, too. Whereas for older generations, a leopard doesn't change its spots, as the saying goes.

We've already discussed people's natural tendency of people to dislike change. To stick with the known rather than the unknown. This ever-polarising view of new things poses a threat to the ability of older generations to inspire younger ones. Rather than reject their interest in new technology, the senior members of society must acknowledge and embrace those things they do not understand in order to fulfil their responsibilities towards the society of the future. It is difficult to inspire young people when older generations carry a distance and disdain for their careers and life trajectories. Older generations can inspire younger ones by understanding that their enthusiasm towards new technology is highly advantageous for their career prospects. People often succeed when working on something that they love and have passion for. But they need leaders, guidance and mentors to help them realise their potential. It is therefore vitally important that older generations offer encouragement and not hindrance.

Who inspires you?

Ideally, everyone would grow up in a supportive family setting where parents, uncles, aunts and grandparents help younger family members navigate through childhood, adolescence, young adult life and beyond. I understand that not everyone is fortunate enough to have that family environment. However, even for those who do, the degree of inspiration available might be limited.

It is therefore often necessary to look to the outside world to reinforce the wisdom offered at home and to optimise it. The internet and social media have their flaws and dangers, yet they also greatly improve access to information and education for anyone with an internet connection or smartphone. Today there is a wealth of resources available for knowledge-sharing and inspiration.

Whether it be through forums, blogs, vlogs (video blogs) or social mediums such as LinkedIn, Twitter, Instagram and so on, there are people out there who regularly share information about how to maximise growth potential and achieve dreams. Seek out those who inspire you the most and learn not only about what they achieved but how they did it. And one common theme about all of them? They all failed, over and over.

Here are some of my favourite sources of inspiration:

Dwayne 'The Rock' Johnson: a former professional American footballer who was rejected by the sport and went on to become a champion professional wrestler, actor, producer, sports franchise owner and all-around awesome guy. He frequently posts about his hard work, hustle and accomplishments on social media, but he also demonstrates how to enjoy a good life and make time for the most important things – family, friends and self. His 'hardest worker in the room' motto might be a little out of reach for some, but his inspiring quality is to put in the maximum effort to achieve his dreams.

Tej Lalvani: CEO of nutraceutical company Vitabiotics and former BBC Dragon on *Dragon's Den*, a television programme in the UK that sees aspiring entrepreneurs pitch business ideas to accomplished entrepreneurs for their investment. I've referenced Tej previously in this book, but his regular LinkedIn posts really help to keep me grounded.

Tej Lalvani · 3rd+ + Follow ···

CEO of Vitabiotics & Dragon on BBC's Dragons' Den (2...

8mo ·

I firmly believe that our biggest enemies in life are self-doubt and an unwillingness to take risks and face challenges.

One key aspect of having a growth mindset is to embrace challenges and view them as opportunities for growth. It's natural to feel intimidated or hesitant when faced with a new task or obstacle, but the key is to not let fear hold you back.

Instead, approach challenges with curiosity and a willingness to learn. Ask questions, seek feedback, and don't be afraid to make mistakes. Remember that failure is not the end, but rather a stepping stone on the path to success.

It's also important to surround yourself with people who encourage and support your growth. Seek mentors and colleagues who challenge you and push you to be your best self.

Ultimately, having a growth mindset means being open to new experiences and continuously striving to improve.

It's about embracing the journey of personal and professional development, and never being complacent with where you are.

629 45 comments · 30 reposts

Credit: LinkedIn: Tej Lalvani

Arnold Schwarzenegger: bodybuilder, actor, politician and The Terminator. I'm subscribed to Arnie's daily newsletter because it's loaded with tips on how to live a healthy and positive life:

'The joy of life is seeing how much more we are capable of doing, and battling so that who we are tomorrow is better than who we are today. Live your life with the curiosity to see what your body and mind can really do, and the knowledge that you'll never really know how much you can accomplish if you don't create a limit. If you do this, I promise you'll feel more fulfilled.'

Credit: Arnold Schwarzenegger: Arnold's Pump Club Newsletter

Jack Ma: Alibaba founder. One of the most successful entrepreneurs in the world, Jack Ma was rejected by thirty different employers after leaving school. He says, *'I even went to KFC when it came to my city. Twenty-four people went for the job. Twenty-three were accepted. I was the only guy who wasn't.'*

Ursula Burns: former CEO of Xerox, multiple non-executive board member and the first African American to be CEO of a Fortune 500 company. Ursula Burns started at Xerox as an intern before becoming an assistant. In this role, she spent much time around senior members of the company's executive management. She was promoted to VP of Global Manufacturing and led the team that delivered Xerox's network printers found in most offices around the world. She says, *'Dreams do come true, but not without the help of others, a good education, a strong work ethic, and the courage to lean in.'*

Carlos Cuesta: assistant manager and individual development coach at Arsenal Football Club, a soccer team in the UK. Carlos Cuesta broke the mould as a soccer coach because he lacked a professional playing career before he took roles at some of Europe's top football clubs, including Atletico Madrid, Juventus and Arsenal. He is just twenty-five years old at the time of writing. He studied sports science in Madrid before embarking around Europe, knocking down doors and bringing the best out of players wherever he works.

Not everyone is going to become a world-famous superstar despite having the potential to do so. It may not be your goal or mission. You may come from a background that will make it really difficult for you to achieve some of the things these megastars have accomplished. I'm personally OK with not being a megastar, and maybe you are too. But even if that's what you want, you'll find many 'rags to riches' stories among the rich and famous. I have used examples from public figures simply because their stories are the most accessible for all.

Rather than fame, it might be that you want to navigate to a management position at a company or some other senior role or become head chef at a popular restaurant in your city. Or you might want to try a variety of careers and be looking for the courage to pursue them. A stark observation I have made when looking into inspirational people is how much their struggles, fears and setbacks resonate with me. They have all had their own challenges to overcome, just like you and I. The differentiating factor is most likely how they responded to them.

These people do not have to share their life lessons with the rest of us. They are busy with a plethora of other priorities. Their words of wisdom are priceless gifts to those of us looking for solutions to the challenges we face in our careers.

Jeff Bezos, Amazon, 1999

Elon Musk, Zip2, 1995

KEY TAKEAWAYS:

In this chapter we talked about inspiration. Where to look for it, who to be inspired by and ensuring we inspire others too. Other key takeaways include:

- Inspiration is the practice of examining both what successes people have and how they got them
- We're surrounded by sources of inspiration. Find and follow those who inspire you
- Failure presents an opportunity to learn and grow – the most inspirational people will tell you how they used their failures to succeed
- Note the distinction between leaders and influencers
- Young people are the future, and we must not stand in their way
- Follow and consume the inspirational material provided by successful public figures because it is easily accessible

Chapter 12

The Next Chapter

I'm not entirely sure why you decided to read this book. Perhaps you're searching for answers to improve your career, or you want to reinforce some of the things you already know. Well done for reading to the end. I wanted you to reach this point because I believe everything that came before it can add value to your career and your life. That is my wish.

Even though you have reached the conclusion of this book, I want you to understand that it is simply the beginning. The beginning of your career, your next chapter or the research you're undertaking before you decide to go after something bold, ambitious and worthy. Whatever is coming next for you, I hope you've found something here that helps you reset and direct your mind to wherever it needs to be.

The material you have read was written to help you look at your career through a different lens without being caught in the whirlwind of the present moment. Perspective is the step back we all need to take from time to time to see how far we've come and how far we have to go to achieve success. It also helps to assess what we've done wrong and what we need to improve.

Chances are, if you're going through something difficult, many thousands of others are going through or have gone through the same or similar. Many of those people stumbled just like you are now. None of them took the express road to success because the journey is littered with setbacks and difficulties. The express road does not exist. The ones who made successes out of their careers resolved to accomplish that success in the face of the adversities they encountered.

If you're at the start of your career, pursue the right experiences that will help you grow and improve in what you're doing. Be authentically and unapologetically yourself. People will respect you for it. Be kind to your colleagues and observe when your ego is serving you well and when it is not. Listen only to advice from people who have earned the right to give it to you. Be brave and take risks when self-doubt is making you question yourself. Learn the many techniques available out there to look after yourself and those close to you, physically and mentally. Seek inspiration from your leaders so you can become one and inspire those around you, too.

As you make your way on your journey, look for the ladders that will help you climb closer to your goals, and accept that behind the next corner might be a setback. Enjoy the process and find happiness. Real happiness. Try not to spend too much time in the future or the past because it's impossible to be in any other place than where you are right now.

'Success is not a destination, but the road that you're on. Being successful means that you're working hard and walking your walk every day. You can only live your dream by working hard towards it. That's living your dream.'

Marlon Wayans

About The Author

James Taylor is a seasoned business professional with over 15 years' experience in both public and private sectors, at small, medium and large companies. He has worked both as an employee and a consultant, and is passionate about harnessing the culture of the workplace, elevating the careers of those he works alongside.

In this book he has consolidated his broad personal knowledge of successes and challenges in the Sporting, Financial and FinTech environments into actionable principles which can be applied in multiple career contexts.

Contact: info@mindsetmulti.media

Printed in Great Britain
by Amazon

45574473R00116